T0375176

VISIONS, DARKNESS, AND LIGHT

VISIONS, DARKNESS, AND LIGHT

A Poetry Novel

Douglas Snodgrass

VISIONS, DARKNESS, AND LIGHT
A POETRY NOVEL

Copyright © 2019 Douglas Snodgrass.

All rights reserved. No part of this book may be used or reproduced by any means, graphic, electronic, or mechanical, including photocopying, recording, taping or by any information storage retrieval system without the written permission of the author except in the case of brief quotations embodied in critical articles and reviews.

This is a work of fiction. All of the characters, names, incidents, organizations, and dialogue in this novel are either the products of the author's imagination or are used fictitiously.

iUniverse books may be ordered through booksellers or by contacting:

iUniverse
1663 Liberty Drive
Bloomington, IN 47403
www.iuniverse.com
1-800-Authors (1-800-288-4677)

Because of the dynamic nature of the Internet, any web addresses or links contained in this book may have changed since publication and may no longer be valid. The views expressed in this work are solely those of the author and do not necessarily reflect the views of the publisher, and the publisher hereby disclaims any responsibility for them.

Any people depicted in stock imagery provided by Getty Images are models, and such images are being used for illustrative purposes only. Certain stock imagery © Getty Images.

ISBN: 978-1-5320-7898-9 (sc)
ISBN: 978-1-5320-7899-6 (hc)
ISBN: 978-1-5320-7900-9 (e)

Library of Congress Control Number: 2019914603

Print information available on the last page.

iUniverse rev. date: 09/19/2019

Very special thanks to God, my dad, my two sons, Bram Stoker, Mary Shelley, Edgar Allen Poe, Boris Karloff, Bela Lugosi, Vincent Price, Stephen King, Dean Koontz, Hawthorne, and all of the great poets.

Special thanks also to Earl Thomas, Mya Barr, Christine Colborne, Deb Speers, and all of the great people of iUniverse; without all of these people, this novel would have never seen the light of day. And especially thanks to my Jedi master, Dina Joyce. Love you, Dina!

Thank you to all of the police officers and firemen who put their lives at risk every day. God bless us all, Tiny Tim! And never forget our brave soldiers.

Darkness, visions, and light. This is a poetry novel and included a short story, "Ouijawa."

Some individual poems are dedicated to certain people.

Visions, Darkness and Light

I wake up to the sounds of fear drifting through life's atmosphere. Cold winds of change assail my soul—such a mystery for one to behold. I see a dream within my mind. So lost, so afraid, and so far behind. A simple answer to my question: Am I just a child of life's rejection? Light that shines so far away. Like lightning on life's stormy days. A broken spell that still remains. It casts dark shadows upon my breath. Once again I'm in life's test. Scream from deep within the night. Oh, so close! Yet out of sight. The deepest stare into the void—truly the most paranoid. Thickest skin that one can wear. Why the hell should someone care? Slip slides into that darkest place. My minds drifting into outer space. On some distant world so full of zombies. The holy shotgun becomes a part of me. I cannot cry so far from home. I'll send instead my evil clone. A life betrayed, into my life's grave. This life I lead that has been saved. Just a test in time beyond this realm. This mortal life will be my hell. A solemn hope within the night, the raven takes his final flight. "Nevermore!" he cries alone. As you slip into life's twilight zone. Come on in child, have a chair. The clowns are scheming—you'd best beware! Staring through the looking glass. And these things too shall also pass.

Drowning in your deepest dream, a demon haunts you as you scream. You've done burned through the sands of time. A whispered wisp that's so sublime. A tale's been told so long ago, it seems you never had a throne. And all you do is wail and moan. Your flesh is stripped down to your bones. Fake crown of fiction is cast aside. Another day to tell your lies. Yet your mind is paralyzed. But now you'd better beware of the evil silence everywhere. Just a short path to your grave, where you become like those depraved. Myself and I, my only friends, we coconspire with the wind. Such a far cry from one's destiny. An excuse to spill that blood you bleed. Suicide of some twisted life, stabbing your own self with that knife. When the devil makes a new disease, he is triumphant and so very pleased.

Now I see this golden rule, like the nuns' narcissistic tool. Stare toward heaven, seems so far away. You're the only one who's left to blame. Somewhere out there, I lost my mind. And now I fall so far behind. So sad to say your truth's not true. That's a lie to me—from inside you. Always trying to find a way back home, but on this world a nomad roams. So much more now has slipped so far away. Tomorrow is already yesterday. Shadow vampires are always chasing me, whispering my name and trying to enslave me. I'm seeing visions in the darkness, revealing where my heart is. Childhood dreams are so elusive; they make my life so inconclusive. If this all seems so damned confusing, I hold to life oh so loosely. Eternal dreams from a forgotten past, you must live each day as if it was your last.

Faintly a whisper, and I hear my angel pray as I drift so far away. I feel forgotten on the bottom; then I look up and see that I've not been. The sorrows make me weep inside, and then I want to run and hide. In death's valley, way far down below, an old witch moans as she loses her soul. Then I jump and run again—just keep on running until the end. The darkness falls, and yet it stays. Once you are gone, you will have no name. Yesterday seems like years ago. Like some fairy tale from days of old. When I feel forgotten, I drift away. Under my breath, I hope and pray.

The bridges we must all cross. Always searching yet still lost. And in my former glory days, I looked and wondered, so amazed. You dream to own your very soul—such a miracle to behold. A wounded child upon life's stage, so far from home and so disengaged. Truth remains within ones grasp; it can be quite deadly as an asp. A future time, so long ago. That's where I dig my deepest hole. In isolation this story remains. I pray to God that my demons are slain. You are so deep within a violation, and all that you own is deep frustration. The blood on your hands remains unexplained, and now you own these unwashable stains. Heart is now fading so deep and fast. Each breath you draw could be your last. Voices in the shadows, calling you by name. Who could it be—or are you insane? A simple life of such simple things. Just like Gollum in *The Lord of the Rings*. Fall down to this earth like its broken slave. Worn down and beaten, yet you still misbehave. That title of arrogance—you wear it so well, it will burn with you in the bottom of hell. Tales of dark possession encircle your camp. A gypsy's curse—that's where you are at! Through some religion or sorcery, they don't really know just what they believe. Like some life you left behind, someone stupid is leading the blind.

All of these dreams shall also pass, just like some long forgotten past. Drowning in the darkest dream, like a rerun on the TV screen. I've seen this show ten thousand times, and still I'm screaming in my mind. A stranger in a stranger land. The more you receive, the more you demand. And when you have finally come and gone, salvation's near; it won't be long. A shadow cried upon my floor. Like Poe's raven, he cried, "Nevermore!" But now that he feeds the rich and devours the poor, that filthy raven exists no more.

Marcia

To Marcia West.

A golden girl from golden days, she was my baby yesterday. We walked through shadows hand in hand. So young and so short on plans. We drifted apart, so lost in life. Still in love yet so far above. An angel spreads his wings, and then he sings. But he could not save me from myself. Flying toward the sun, like Icarus I fell. That golden girl passed me by. The only thing that I cared about was nothing deep inside. Years back then were moving slow, so I still saw her to and fro. I thought to myself, *Somehow, somewhere.* Yet it seemed that I did not care. Like the wind, I drifted away, and then I would hear her name and stop to pray.

The years got faster every day; still, now and then I'd stop and think. This woman I've loved so very long; the path I chose so very wrong. And I'd wonder how her life had been and then I saw her once again. It brought my past to here and now. But yes, so childish I was. Oh, yes! And how! Nothing turned out as we had once dreamed' a self-made illusion, it did seem. Yet those memories kept me warm.

Douglas Snodgrass

Every now and then, that dream's reborn. I've always loved her since forever. So sweet, so shy, yet very clever. So this poem I write for her. It's so much less than she deserves.

The Mummy

He was a king of Egypt old. A million slaves lifted up his throne. They chiseled his likeness into stone. By his own pride, he was overthrown. Killed so many so far and wide, with all of his sorcerers by his side. That he was emperor was not denied. A lost well of souls he did devise. He marched against all ancient kings. His army killed them in their dreams and mastered almost everything, from sea to sea and in between. Sands like blood ran through his veins. God's own angels knew his name.

So sure that his legacy would remain, he lost himself along the way, betrayed by all that he trusted most. Even his queen was deception's host. Destroyed his flesh and yet cursed his ghost. In his own sarcophagus he would roast; time marches on under life's sun. It starts to crawl, and then it runs. Years all finally seem like a month. A whispered wish, and then it's done. Those desert sands, they blow and blow—and hide your corpse so deep below. That which you reaped, you also sowed. Discord upon all of hell's below. Preserved and waiting for some new life. Curse etched upon your tomb, for all eyes. Man's own greed, his own demise.

And then he acts oh so surprised! Stories have been told for some thousand years to enslave the future of man's fears and destroy all that you hold so dear. You think this choice would be crystal clear.

The treasure hunter comes to take, but Tutankhamen he will awake. He kills the sheep and feeds the snake. And now this demon's curse you will partake. Oh, such ignorance they do conceive, these simple men who do not believe. When their time comes, they shall flee and deny their own apostasy. Then they desecrate your tomb. Would've been better to crawl inside their mothers' wombs. You will see his shadow upon the moon. And now you know that he is coming soon. Somewhere in the sands of time, some will live, yet most will die. You have no wings on which to fly, do you have to run and hide.

Now this demon prowls this earth. In his rage of hell's rebirth, upon your blood he does thirst. Of all the plagues, he is the worst. And in this dark hypocrisy, men will die. And, yes, they will bleed. Their own self-destruction they will feed, to be cast as stones beneath his feet.

He'll be wrapped in linens from the grave. The two beside him, his favorite slaves from the land of the lost and depraved. Some will fall beneath his blade. He holds your life within his hands and will bury your soul beneath the sands. There is for you no promised lands. Your breath and soul is his demand. A cry from way down deep below—that's where the end is dark and cold. So long ago, this story was told. You will pay this demon sevenfold. Run fast, child, lest you be enslaved. You are this hunter's only prey. For those secret sins, you will finally pay. Upon the dust your flesh remains. This monster will not ever pretend. He was the pharaoh of his land. Built his throne on the back of man. This mummy here that you see is a part of you, and pieces of me. To send him back down to his place without a sign, and with no trace, a monster sleeping in the sand. To awake and rule once again. The mummy will betray your flesh. The soul he seeks will seem so fresh. Before you send him back to hell, lock him down at the bottom of the well. He kicks and screams as he burns. And then he feeds those hungry worms—the mummy.

Prologue

Between the edges of reality lies a thin line full of insanity. And the truth and what lies so far beyond. Some ordinary day, I will just sing along. And that day becomes a place, where I can hide behind my face. This mask that I wear—what does anyone care? Does your neighbor share? Or shun you all alone, casting that first stone?

Between gray and the dawn, a different world goes on. Take such a simple mind to see all this chaos inside of me. It melts into a fade. It's darkness as it's made. Forever this life's slave, a victim self-made?

Calamity is a part of this life; its drama cuts like a sharpened knife. This world and all of its daily strife, it does not matter in our afterlife. So sit back down and enjoy this ride.

Another Day

To Chris Harriss Barbee.

Mesmerized by the innocent, alone and wondering upon my way. I reached into this afterlife, so far beyond this grave. These years pass on by, and they barely dull the pain. You are so far away, and I needed you here today. Now I'm so lonely, lost, and cold—sad and so afraid. Barely one day passes by, and still you have come and gone. There are many things I have done right, but so many more that I have done wrong. Those things I find I cherish most have been there all along. This prayer I pray for you today. It makes me feel that I belong. One breath upon my life's wind, I sing its sullen song. Never realized, my friend, that I would have to let you go. Didn't really know how much I loved you, bro. The hand of fate took you to the other side. A part inside of me, inside that same day, also died. How much time since I've cried, and how really hard that I have tried. And a part of me still feels denied. It's so cold again, in life's winter wind, as I remember you, my friend. In some other time, in another place, this song would never end. Done lost myself along life's way. I had some words left to say. Fall down to my knees, hope and pray. That's where we will meet on another day. In another place, as this one fades away. This promise that I've made: we will meet on another day, on another day. Another day.

Poltergeist

The attic is knocking at my door. Been through this experience before. Got angels gathered around my grave. There is a part of me that you cannot save. So much of this story has done been told. And now this story is stealing my soul. God's revenge is sevenfold. Lost and alone, been dead and gone to myself for so very long. Ethereal spirits that call out my name so naughty, full of mischief. I'm not alone. They came alive in the darkness, full of grief and sadness. Spiritual tomes from some other dimension. They read like self-help books for demon possession. Hold on to yourself and don't slip away. Those angels still gather around my grave. The supernatural is ice-cold in my veins. Whispers from shadows driving me insane. My mind is paralyzed, and I cannot decide. A poltergeist from the corner of my mind's eye. They don't cure any illness, and they screech at the blind. There is a poltergeist right next to me. Another parasite that feeds on the blood that I bleed. A poltergeist is my only friend, taking me to the devil's end.

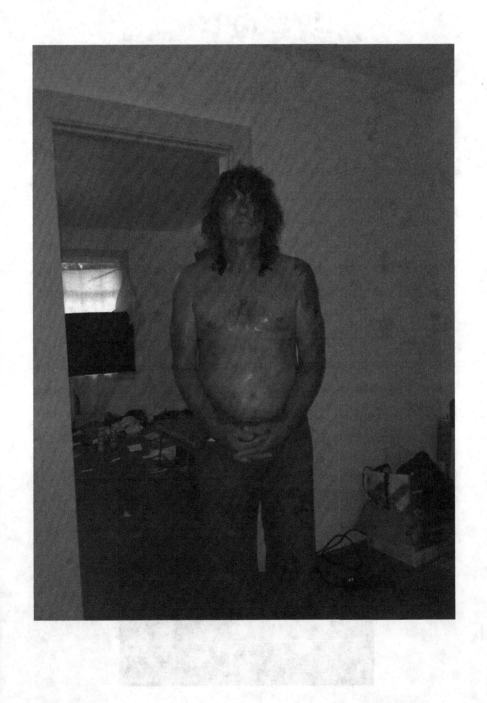

Hope

Whispering winds that lazily toil through the graveyard trees. Open flight of nocturnal, on darkness they all feed. Clouds of madness and despair, suffering in quiet ecstasy. From an open wound pours all of the blood that's left to bleed. A sigh from deep within, the earth is made to groan. An empty, sullen mystery, reaping what is sown. A precious, single moment, awake and all alone. A falling shooting star, so deep in the unknown. Sadness in the sky, a sign from far above. Just an ordinary angel, full of light and love. That heart was torn away, and pain is not enough. Sufferings of the silent the only ones that you can trust. So go forward, smile, and know that there is one more day. And now you must believe. Just close your eyes and pray.

Untitled #1

This calm before life's storm always seems to carry on. But in your darkest hour, so weak and all alone, I pray for power as I walk in this unknown. Way down below, as I fly high, on these wings I will win—or execute myself. There are no guarantees except heaven, hell, or death. Think all things through before your last breath. You might get high on everything, just to make you see we're all the same. Always looking for someone else to blame. Denial is the cornerstone to defeat and a rebirth of catastrophe. Just like a sign from God. We've spoiled the children and spared the rod. And now there will be hell to pay. Because the devil will have his day.

Freak Show

The freak show is coming to town; got Nosferatu and a very evil clown. Price for admission is free. The demon inside pays for you and me. The got methamphetamines and anything else you need. All at Ariel's freak show, that fire is burning way down below. For a song and a dance, you can die for one day. And if you like it, you can choose to stay. Get down on your knees! To your God you will pray! Just one more line; it's time to do your time. Ladies and gentlemen, can I have your attention, please? Form a line for every symptom and disease. Step right up! We've got what you need! Does not even matter if you even believe, when the freak show comes to town. It takes every drop of blood you have left to bleed, even those ones you need. That clown is laughing at you and me.

Bring Hellfire Down

Destroyed all of my dreams of yesterdays. They are all taking me to life's end. Victimized by ten million lies. That are all burying me in my sins. Mind taken by force and indoctrinated. Ultra secret, all so intrusive. It's just as thin as the wind but so much more elusive. Left me out in hell's own wilderness to live or die on my own. Now I am your own personal terrorist, and I'm going to kill you and your evil clone. I'm laying my own law down. I'm a super synchronized tragedy of all of that is humanity. I'm gonna bring hellfire down. A show that shows you a new definition for insanity. Bringing all of hell's fire down. I'm gonna burn your ass to the ground. Imprisoned me inside of myself, freedom to slavery. Darkness my only friend. Sadducees and Pharisees sniffing outside of my door. *Take me far away,* I prayed into the wind. A prisoner of illusion, burning hate. Dark forces all-inclusive. Like witches casting evil spells. Sick love for the abusive.

Forest with Fairies

Pale butterflies rise in ominous clouds above this yellow-brick dream. Dyslexic dawn lies broken in the west. Amid my nightmares, a scream. Goliaths have swords to wield. And one more gathers to this feast. Because the great will become the least. So very humble, and so meek. One different day, and just one more song. I will pray that we all just sing along. Those birds of prey, so full of hate. It is my soul that they denigrate. A simple life that does deceive. So full of lies and mockery. This naked bleeding forest that you see—it's outside of you and coming for me. These jaded fairies are a lost magic race, and they can put you in your permanent place. In this forest, so extraordinary. Just to live through each day is oh, so scary! Canary in the coal mine. This evil beside me, it's the moment that most would fade. Am I so far lost that I cannot be saved? This tree that lives beside me breathes just as I breathe. My life at its mercy as it watches me sleep. This grass beneath my feet talks softly in my sleep. And such sweet dreams this all makes. And I'm still dreaming wide awake. Like an eclipse upon my soul, in that crystal ball you so tightly hold. That life itself leads to infinite sadness and buries you in a hurricane of madness. But like the feral animals in the forest, all know there is a time to rest and a time to go. They leave this home within their land; this I do not understand. This breath we breathe is not for free. Like fairy dust shines down on me. And now those visions are oh, so real! They teach me how to think and feel. And when I slip and fade away, a falling star will light my way. A pilgrim's journey somewhere in time. I'm still stumbling, alone and blind. In this life or the next, a little hope is all that is left. Ethereal spirits that guard this realm, with Captain Howdy at the helm. A night owl screeched its eternal question. Is this providence, or random selection? This forest is alive on every level of its being. The most amazing things are the things that you are not seeing. A snarl, a hiss, a songbird in flight. A serene, cold death upon your darkest night. These slithering, creeping, crawling things. They seem they're on most everything. Blind fear and hunger take their toll as parasites gnaw at your soul. Have you, poor child, done lost your way? You pray to see a new light's day? A sharp cold blows beneath the wind. The forest sees all of your secret sins. These fairies rule upon their throne. No time or space, all so all alone. A distant tragic sudden spell, trapped inside a wishing well. And here we go around and around, you will be lost and never found. There is no one here who wears a crown. The higher you go, the deeper that you drown. The fairies could feed upon your flesh, but first you must pass their final test. If you truly do survive, you've only made it through one night. Pray for mercy, for your own soul as your final life unfolds. Life is so contrary, in this forest with fairies.

Leave This All Behind

A whispered dream from down deep inside—that's where I go when I run and hide. Doesn't matter how hard I have tried, these millions of tears I've cried. I must always still decide to live in the darkness or the light. Tomorrow has no answers; too many questions left behind. This life that I have chosen is so very hard to find. As I fade into the twilight and feel that I've gone blind, an illusion from the wishing well interrogates my mind. How many visions must I see? How many religions must I believe? How many decisions must I need? It's so hard to breathe. I'm so really tired, and I need to sleep, just for a little while. A tale's been told ten thousand times. That's where I live my life, on the edge of a razor knife. I choose to follow that light; it seems so warm and bright. And if I should die tonight from some malfunction deep inside, and when the truth becomes a lie, no one is left who can decide. How many stories must I read? How many terrors must I see? How many issues must I feed? It's so really hard to feel. And I just need to sleep for a little while. How many roads must I travel? What will happen if I unravel? How much more pain can I handle? I see a flickering light from a distant candle. I am tired and just need to sleep for a little while. I'm not looking for the answers to any questions left behind. Just get one more chance to prove myself; then I will leave this all behind. Before I lose what's left of my mind, just leave this all behind. And I'm tired and just need to sleep for a little while.

Dust

I have been wrong for so long that I think I am insane. All of these visions in the darkness, they are all calling me by name. So much has slipped away; tomorrow is yesterday. Live in this life for just a little while, just for a dream and a few quick smiles. Then just like dust, I will blow away. And then there is nothing left to say. I've turned to dust along life's way. A million more will come like me, and like the ocean's tide, they will recede.

The Lycan

It was a full October moon, back in 62. In Israel, land of the Jews, I became a little bit confused. In the shadow of some devil's lair, I could feel the chaos in the air. But no one could much explain this future source of their dying pain. I heard a low growl on the wind. It made the hair raise on my skin. This temple courtyard I'm beside. I feel the need to run and hide. It seemed part man but was a wolf. So evil and mean, so long in tooth. Its eyes bloodred like an open wound. I prayed to God that he didn't smell me soon. Creeping and crawling in my retreat, so silent that I could not squeak. I dropped into the labyrinth of tunnels below, into a vague darkness that I did not know. I had no light to find my way, but I had to move; I could not stay. Slowly down this darkest trail, hoped that I was escaping hell. It twisted and turned into the earth. I tripped and fell and lay so still. A small scratching sound that I so faintly heard. Devoid of all light, the darkness was blurred. I dared barely even breathe; the darkness covered me like some snake's outer skin. The sweat came down, so deep within. I closed my eyes and began to pray. That was when I heard a slight noise made. It made my skin crawl to the bone. That was when I realized that I was not alone. No one heard my scream so deep in the earth. I did bleed. Upon my flesh it fed so well. Not much was left that one could tell. This labyrinth was my tomb. It was my choice; no one else to blame. I crucified my very soul at the open gate to hell's crossroads.

Bedouin

Where the poppies grow in the mountain fields is where the Bedouin spirits drift through time and space. One thousand years of deep tradition, these so-called masters of our human race. A wail and moan as the full moon rises and then falls. Caves full of demons and darkness; death lies beyond the city walls. The winding path to perdition starts with your forgotten dreams. Danger so real and rewards so few, with no understanding of what it all means. Standing at the crossroads in an ancient mountain pass. One leads to safety, one leads to uncertainty—and the other to certain death. The spirits watch you pick and choose, hoping to steal your last breath. A cold, hard land for a ship of fools. Crashing their *Titanic* into the River Styx. The Bedouin spirits are here to guide you home; your soul is on their list. And now you are a nomad too. There is no more redemption for you.

Loyal Soldier

*For all who fought and returned, and especially
for the fallen who were left behind. The fifty-eight
thousand plus, and our allies. God bless them all.*

The jungle is so dark and so big. A machine gunner's nest
hiding deep within. We had retaken this hill so many times;
I'd lost count of the number of men who had died. Snakes
that slither, and the creatures of the night. It all keeps you
on edge as the nocturnal take flight. Inch by inch we push
forward toward the great unknown. Though other soldiers
are present, you feel so all alone. A crackle, a snap, and they
all stood so still. There was sweat on their brows; a slight fear
they did feel. After a moment, they heard no more noise and
sent a scout forward. They were still paranoid. They heard
the squeal of a wild pig and were almost relieved, but waited
for the scout before they would proceed. Heard the pin exit
some random grenade. Bright flash straight up ahead. No
one had to ask; they knew that scout was dead. Lightning
strafing through the sky, their backs against the wall. They
had no choice except to fight, or take the risk of losing them
all. They dug themselves into the ground and became their
deaths' imminent resistance. They tossed grenades of their

own and with their .308s tried to mow them down. But in a forest it knew all too well, the enemy was like a bloodhound. A standoff they barely had at best, at the bottom of hell, staring at their graves. The lieutenant was the second man down, next in command, then took the reins. It was just a moment in life's madness, when everything's just going insane. Killing the people in this foreign land for reasons no one fully understands. You give your life and give your soul to the reaper's thin disguise. A hero's death you will obtain. But with the politicians, no honor remains. It was such a sad moment in time. Seven kept their lives that day. Nobody knows how, but everyone was praying. And there is an old saying: It rains on the just and the unjust.

Guardian Angel

For my mother.

When I was just a young boy, I felt so safe in Mother's arms. I believed that she would save me from the monsters, that they could do me no harm. Such a treasured moment in my life. It's been ten years plus since she went to sleep. Now I'm a lonely older man, those memories all of the treasures that I keep. If I hurt myself, she felt my pain. She had such a gentle, giving soul. When I was sad, she made me smile. Put a blanket on me when I slept so cold. I got so sick I thought I'd die, but chicken broth, aspirin, and Mother's love were the cure. For a while I was left on my own as I grew into a troubled young man, so unsure. Those prayers she prayed were never wasted, though sometimes I think that she thought they were. A blackened hole lay in place of my soul, killing my desire to be anything. Just a random rolling stone because it gathers no moss and has no roots of its own. Drifting so far away, all alone, so far that I'd lost my way back home. She was my fire in life's winter storm. Please, Mother, deliver me into God's holy hands so I can make my way into the promised land and rest in eternity with my guardian angel.

Alexander

On the rise, an enormous military machine. The reality that Phillip's son became the king. Stretched out his hand against all foreign lands. Took other thrones for his kingdom, owned them as his own. Nothing less, yet nothing more. Risk giving your life at the edge of his sword. Horses of iron and warriors so valiant. A death driven, unrelenting from his stallion. And the awesome army that surrounded him. Alexander, what did you see in those visions that you received? You knew your destiny; you and Hephaestion always knew. Had the whole known world within your grasp. As we shall see, his legacy still lasts. Alexander, king and master of everything. Now, you still feel his touch today; that influence still remains. Alexander proved that he was second to none and, in his time and place, God's chosen one. He united the world beneath his fist and accomplished everything upon his list. He died so young, his mission completed. All that stood in God's way were tamed or defeated. Alexander the Great. A large statue in your honor as your soul forever floats upon the River Styx.

Shadows

There was a wisp of whispering; it was all beyond a veil of nothing. A cry upon the open sky. I cannot see, for I am blind. An empty chasm of hypocrisy. The deeper you cut, the harder I bleed. And then I'm empty; it's dark and cold. I feel my soul migrating into shadows. It's where I find comfort from judgment called down on me. If you would just leave your number, I will customize your disease. But you never had a basic clue; your cover-up was harder than the truth, just a shadow in life's wind. We're all falling down a well of sin. Please tell me when to stop and where to begin, because I'm living beyond shadows, down some long forgotten dusty road, just trying to find my way back home. My life driven like cold Alaskan rain into the shadows.

Oxy's

I was born under a moon of disposition, like my father's life's deepest tradition. Now I see across this ghostly dimension. I wail beside the moon, "Have I earned your attention?" In my best intentions, such a small thing I should not even mention. Now I'm finding my way back to the other side, just like wasting away in my afterlife. Scratch until I bleed, so much confusion that I don't need. Just need to smile as I awaken; too many truths have been forsaken. Sometimes I feel my heart as it is breaking. Wonder if my life is laying naked. In a breeze upon heaven's gates, it's another truth we will investigate. I feel my future is so close at hand. I already lived it out yesterday. Turn the hourglass over one more time. A single moment that was lost in side. That's where I'll hide until I die. The cost of killing the pain, the reason you're high.

Estranged

I tried to call your phone, but you are never there. Worry about you all of the time, but you just don't seem to care. A picture is worth a thousand words; I see it all so clear. We have drifted so far apart, yet we were never near. I always pray for you at night, all alone, wondering what you are doing, in my melancholy zone. Promised many things to you; I failed at some. But I've never failed to smile into the rising sun. You have pushed me far away, and now the absence makes me colder. I am getting older, and soon I will be on my way. But you will no longer have me here to cast me aside once again. I will not give a damn about your pain. I will be resting upon the wind. You will miss me one day, but I will not be there for you. This experience that we all call life will forever be through. There is very little time left for me. Your anger so foolish that you can't see. From this mortal flesh, I will break free and see a new son shine that really loves me.

Inez

To my maternal grandmother.

I know that you grew up in such hard times, and that man you'd known was never there. Only God knows how many tears you cried and those sacrifices you gave for four children in your care. Times were kind of tough back in 1962. Not many had real money, but family was true. Such a strong presence upon my life taught me things that still remain. I hope you are treated well in life's afterlife. I still see your tears in the rain. And Grandma, I still feel your pain. And I see your smile upon the wind when I close my eyes and go to sleep. Did the best of the best you could with what you had. That we did not speak one last time makes me so sad. You helped make me the man I am, but you were more than I could ever be. And now you are free. I love you forever, and one day, I pray that you are at peace. I'm down so far upon my knees. A small, still, deep voice from so far inside of me tells me that you are all right. If you can read these words that I wrote for you, I hope you are smiling—and Grandma, I'll see you soon.

Praetorian Guard

A soldier of deep tradition on a mission to a place beyond the wall. He can't let this boneyard hold me down. You have to rise before you fall. Marching down a dead man's trail to find a way back to his family's home. A sword in one hand, a shield in the other. Trying to find glory with Rome. Advance, assault, and a slight retreat. Blood pours upon the thirsty dirt and quickly sours in the heat. Even though he knows no fear, he knows that death is always near. Birds of prey circling in life's atmosphere, waiting for this feast to begin. Everybody has one thought on his mind: to make it to the end and win. This soldier on his noble cause to bring honor to the crown. If this enemy had its way, he would be rotting in the ground. Been trained since youth for this very day. As a Roman soldier, he was no man's slave. He fought so bravely to the end and was gravely wounded. More so dead than alive. But alas! That soldier did survive. Rome won the battle on that day, and a hero's welcome Caesar surely gave. For all had almost shown to be as brave as that one soldier.

Transformation

Swirling, twisting strands of time, sifting down into the bottom of everything. A golden child of man's creation stands at the precipice of some infinite sadness. Black hole in the sun, a doorway to hell. Spirits crossing across dimensions; I smell their faint repetition. Kindly let me know when you reach that destination so I can plan to float upon the wind and set both feet upon the seven seas at the same time. So that the fear of the unknown becomes knowledge and the elixir of your soul intoxicates you as a fine wine on some long ago picnic in a forest dream. The unity of obscurity shows a brand-new path to freedom. And that smile upon God's face reaches out to all of humanity. It's just a character of His kindness, which reminds us to humble down our tomes. No lies can remain, for the truth draws near. And now it's standing at the door.

Goodbye

To Phillip "Rocky" Graham.

Those demons before me are digging a hole with both hands to find a mythical lost world that's so far away. Seems that I can no longer believe in anything. Have to be a supernatural, to be called by my given name. Drifting back into such an innocent time. Me and my high school friend, I see it all once again. I have a faded photograph; we all stood side by side. And not long thereafter, that tragic day that you died. Those angels so very helpless, standing beside you, but it was far too late. That decision had already been made. I can't begin to understand the twisted hand of fate. A slight parallel from inside the underneath of life's darkest secrets. I just have a moment to remember my friend. He took us all to his dark place. It must have been his secret prison cell. I'm falling to this earth with my broken dreams, and velocity is the only thing that I can feel. It's still so surreal and unreal. I'm all alone and crying inside this broken version of your life's dream. I will love you forever, friend, but it's another tragedy. Eternity has claimed you for itself. Goodbye.

Prisoner

I can see what you can't see, even if you look deep down inside of me. The closer you come, the further you will fall until you find that you are confined within the walls. The voices are all inside of my head. Some may be alive, yet most are dead. A special place for you, my friend, because I can tell that you are one of them. You need a tattooed number on your arm. If you resist, we will do you more harm. Inside democracy's hypocrisies. At the bottom of the well, exploring the underlying disease of the absence of your obedience. Surrender at your own risk, or be forgotten, dead and gone forever. Artificial intelligence with a blueprint to your soul. Better quickly flee to the heavens and listen to your secret prayer. The one that leads you to your mother's tomb, so you can crawl inside her empty womb once again and find some kind of solace in your slander of sacrifice. Hidden in your own pretentious slavery of your spirit, under life's sun, you can't be the only one whom I recognize, who's trapped in prison for the rest of your life, just a prisoner.

Haunted Castle

Child with bloodstained eyes, a most eerie apparition. She stands at the top of the broken stairwell, seething with hatred and pain, screaming at the silence. One of many who reside here fades back to life. In the dead of midnight, young boys and girls, murdered for their life's blood. Supposed fountain of youth for an affluent pagan madam. So sadly, Ponce de Leon is himself made a fool. For quite some time, no one knew until so many had been used, those ones that no one could save. Their poor, broken bodies thrown into the catacombs. When she was finally brought to justice, there was nothing left but their naked bones. A few they still saved from a dungeon down below. But so many that were gone; their names would never be known. Her accomplice escaped into the middle of the night. Pied piper of the devil, he led those children to their end. Come time for the price to be paid, he slipped underneath the wind.

They buried them in unmarked graves. Put the aristocrat in jail, locked down in chains. When finally face-to-face with what she had done, her heart could not maintain. She died alone inside her little cell and took many dark secrets with her as well. The castle abandoned and crumbling to the ground. Still at night, you hear the children screaming, and an apparition shows itself. There is no redemption or mercy because that madam burns in hell. That accomplice that she had was a devil all the same. The saddest thing is that no one remembers their names. There is nothing more that we can do to ease their suffering and pain at the haunted castle.

The Murderer

It was a place that I used to play in, though only on rainy days. Where Captain Howdy was my friend, and now he's feeling angry again. I must go forth and take my fill. All those whom I meet, I want to kill. Those clowns are laughing in the rain until nothing else remains. This hell that is deep within my mind, it's all driving me insane. Until the waking of the shadows and your savior in the wind, it's just another means to an end, just a personal sin within your false reality. You hold your breath and barely breathe. Just a lost animal in this place, another disgrace to this human race. A demon took me by the hand. He said, "Come here, son. I'll help you understand." And now you understand hell and death. When will you breathe your last breath? Down into this earth, they lower your flesh. Now eternity begins, and you will have no rest.

A Simple Prayer

For Kristene, my sister.

It seems that I have lost my way in this darkness. Just one breath upon this wind. I don't even know where quite to begin. This deepest, darkest, coldest night—a fear of fear is lost, all alone. I tried to tell you on the telephone. A simple prayer that light's God's path. Just a little bit, where you can see where he's at. Heaven is heaven, forever and beyond. But our mortal life is not so long. Like a mist and then it drifts away; all that is left is to listen and pray. A humble child is the potter's clay. He is so near yet seems so far away. Just a simple prayer that keeps you on my mind. All those truths in life that you embrace. Just seek and you will find. It's just a simple prayer, just a moment of your time. A simple prayer. A lost moment in time.

The Alien

Among those stars up in the sky remains a question: what, who, or why? Does an angel hold in place the sun? Is evolution the answer for everyone? Is Jesus God's one and only son? A face upon the moon, calling out to a child. A random act of kindness, like lost breath upon the wind. Where does it all end? When did this all begin? Stare into the heavens like some lost soul, unafraid. Can't help but think about absolution in the middle of this confusion. Is there some mystical solution? So many planets with so many suns. Do you really believe that we are the only ones? So deep in the night, just staring into the sky. A falling shooting star, so cold and all alone. From the corner of my mind's eye, what lies hidden will be exposed. That which hides in secret is a prophecy unto itself. One day of pain cannot remain. Is there somewhere else that I can go? Is there something else that I should know? Is Area 51 my ancestors' home? A full moon that breathes is reaching out to me. A lost signal from afar, coming through in waves. Beginning to wonder, are we masters or the slaves? Or something else by chance? Maybe just an unfortunate circumstance? Could it all be just so designed? A truth that you cannot see because you are so blind? Am I this alien, or is it you? Is there a path we each must choose? Some lost, forbidden race hidden deep in outer-inner space? This alien that you see in the mirror looks just like me. The alien.

Betrayal

There was a man of madness. He fell into the underworld, became a slave for immortal predators, a familiar within their clan. Worked his way up through the ranks. Became a master of their everything. Worked the slaves to their early graves but brought pleasure to his dark masters. He was longing for immortality, a disciple of abomination. A lost moment in a trajectory of darkness. There was a reluctance to share immortality, and now betrayal was close at hand. Under siege of Christian vigilantes with their crosses, swords, and staves. And now that man of madness is an open grave. His eternal soul an open sepulchre of this world. And now he is just ashes upon life's wind.

The Gladiator

Trained from the time that he was young to be a stone-cold killer of men. Pledged all of his allegiance to Caesar and his animal that lay within. He was just barely a man, a wolf among sheep. And just like an animal, he practiced what he preached. He became a master of the games. He took others' blood for his daily bread. If you were watching him, you'd best watch yourself instead. Because he was already inside your head, and next thing that you know, you are dead. Many scars and so many pains—all just a part of the games. The crowd demanded blood, so drunk on all the violence. They felt no victim's pain, a false illusion of everything. He was the emperor's favorite of all. He answered the animal's call. There was no mercy that he could extend, only blackness in his soul. When the game master takes it all away, hell is your only home. Hand to hand or spear to sword. His might and skill could not be ignored. And when it becomes his day to die, not one tear will leave his eyes. His days all come to him just the same. Maybe just a flutter of doubt inside. But he is an elitist gladiator, so full of homicide. When his days pass, they might write of his fame. More likely it will prove that man is so depraved. There will always be a master over the slave. But the gladiator's chosen his own grave. Just another lost soldier in time, with a little lost piece of everything. That is tearing this world up inside. This gladiator will not be denied.

Lost Moment in Time

I was born just yesterday, and before tomorrow I will pass away. But in between I will break the dawn; my wayward soul must carry on to reach beyond some distant realm beyond your most current dreams. And I am just a ghost upon nothing, like a lost, forgotten moment in time that lies alone of some darkest night till that morning's daylight? A bat flying alone in the darkness, and now you see my darkest secrets. Yes, I cry so late at night, when I see that truth that reveals the story about me and you. Just a little smile, and my shadow floats away. Just like that smile you had yesterday. Was like a ghost walking across my grave. I cannot see past everything. It's just a silent moment in life, before this all just slips away.

Fly Away

Disturbed upon October's day—that was when it all just blew away. Upon my knees, I cried. In loneliness I was so afraid. Cried out in pain; it made me mad. No more chains like once I had. A pair of wings to fly away into a new bright shining day. I'll touch the fire in the sun. Into this darkness I will run. A child alone within a dream. It should not matter, it should seem. The rabbit goes down his hole; if you follow, it could cost your soul. If you stay, it's so empty, cold. Seems a million stories have done been told. In a vision inside your lonely world, a whispered prayer that Jesus heard. Now, it does not matter anyway. With your new pair of wings, you will just fly away. Are you an angel, or the devil's slave? Or just a whisper beyond life's grave?? A clone, perhaps? A disturbing game. When you fly away, no one remembers your name.

Gift

will first move along to her next one.

Girl

One day you are afraid, bad health and chaos once again. Every waking moment in time is another lesson in this life. The underside of everything will show you the real dark world. Make an appointment at your own convenience. You're such a damned genius flailing all around like a puppet on his strings, led by this naughty girl, who is your master. Life is spinning ever faster, and you don't care about anything except a poisoned girl. And now you have gone and fallen into bad times. Just waiting for deliverance, with that devil girl at your side. And she don't even give a damn about her own life. She's just a succubus without any dreams, living at the bottom of life's darkness in a feeding frenzy upon your soul. Just a wicked girl, a wandering nomad, drifting through her filth and lies. Those drugs she takes are no surprise. Before she is done, she will take your life by an overdose of suicide. She's just a girl, a wandering nomad. And when you are gone, she will just move along to her next one.

The Witch

Old lady in the woods who lives all alone. She eats little children and makes jewelry with their bones. Many say that she is a witch, over three hundred years old. Many have tried to take her down, and they also were never found. Frail, cluttered path led the way into a tragic, toxic realm. At the edge of insanity, nothing remains except the rapture of consequence. A fear lingering always in the settlements, and those rumors grew darker each and every year that John Hathorne of Salem's fame had run from her in fear. Those children had never been found. But the carvings from their bones were hanging from the limbs of forlorn trees, like a warning to heroes and heathens before they enter into this world of disbelief. An omen filled with magic spells that will take your soul straight down to hell. But you are lost upon an angry trail and looking to find your salvation. To the other side of a lake of fire. If you close your eyes and pray to believe, you just might make it safely home in the twilight of the morning's light. That ends with that death, that ends with your dream so down deep inside. We are off to never, not ever land. That cold and empty hole—forever it demands that you pay that price in whole as she eats your very soul. An exorcist from the old land came to mete some justice down—and in his own fears he did drawn. A pied piper in the forest puts his spell upon the wind. Praying to a ghost about your life's desire, you cannot get any higher, than you already are. The witch calls out to you in your darkest morning dreams. If you listen closely to the wind, you can hear her victims scream.

So Soon

I live so far away, in the inner recesses of my naked soul. I feel life's winter in my bones; it's a feeling that so few own. I smile upon my whisper, upon life's wind. I'm so glad to be here once again. Answer to your question is I don't know. And the answer to said question is so far down deep below, beneath the seven seas of the sands of time. It all feels so very strange and so sublime. Like a piece of fruit from that sacred place, a life that is lived, that leaves no trace. I stare up at you from my open grave. It is time to pay for all of these mistakes that I have made. But a feather of hope drifts beyond heaven's gates. God is coming for me, another exiled actor from this world's stage. Though I have gone so far away, a memory lives on. It's from me to you, and now I will see you so soon.

Jackie Light

Another black cloud spins over my head.

Like some boomer story from down deep inside. This earth keeps on spinning long after I'm dead.

And I still have no answers to my question: Why? If I could work on water, I wouldn't need Jesus. If I could heal myself, I would be immortal. Anything for the spoiled child that it pleases. I falter as my heart starts to tremble.

I start to pray beneath my breath. Is this my Lord's greatest test? This life I've owned, now I must decide: take my soul to hell or paradise?

Magic mirror on the wall, save us from us all. This pain down so deep inside, I want you to feel it just one night. And while you dream of suicide, I will be hanging right by your side. A spell is cast upon us all. It feed those demons inside that crawl. The cathedral bells tolls, and my spirit folds into this catastrophe name humanity. I agree to disagree, you well disciplined across my knee. These sad faces that you see are that reflection in your soul, an empty soul, insanity. Just one chance to bleed you down. Six fucking feet beneath this ground.

I stare at you with open my eyes, these pennies removed from my eyes. Under bloodred skies, now I say goodbye to my friend Jackie's light.

Jesse James

He had two six-guns strapped down to his side. An all alone outlaw obsessed with homicide. Rob, cheat, and kill—his chosen occupation. And with a small guerrilla war gang, he had his own operation. There were people who wanted him dead, so he had to drift to stay alive. In the wild, hard west, you did your best just to survive. You made your bed with a saddle for a pillow. Drinking that moonshine, sometimes a lot was just a little. But like all things do, it comes with its price, and you hope each day that it will be all right. But you can't look back, childhood innocence cast aside. It's almost too late to run and hide. A hangman's noose overshadows your dreams, and you hear that rattlesnake as its tail sings. Some days so cold, wet, and hungry, it can be so dark and lonely, living in a brief moment in history. Civil War done took anything that you cared about anyway. Now you lead a dysfunctional anomaly with your brother's help—such a notorious family. In 1868, they took their own highway to the devil. Fame or fortune? Like perfect criminal poetry in motion. Cole Younger, with his brothers, the devil's consort. But Jesse James had the brains to walk that outlaw way, and he never bowed to no one, not even now, today. Those who live by the sword will die by the sword. And you may rest assured only a ghost of his voice is heard anymore. But to hear that cannon roar, the devil's voice in that .44, it will take you to some secret place, hidden in those valleys below, where the hidden rivers run so full of blood and mother's milk will flow. And all of Texas and hell lies before you as your anger becomes your favorite sin. Looking through that window at your grave, do you finally realize that you are just another slave searching for some long lost holy grail, just another nail on your coffin to beat on? Jesse James, a true American icon, lived his life on its most slippery edge. Then he slipped six feet into his coffin, and all that anger is burning with Jesse forever.

The Resurrection

Sunday, April 1, 2018

He rode into the most holy city, full of love and forgiveness.
They welcomed him like a conquering hero. In the blink of
one eye, they villainized his holiness. The Sadducees and
Pharisees believed in themselves more. Though their souls
were black and so full of hate, they called it loving-kindness
in the deep depths of their insanities. Fear and darkness
and uncertainty were the salvations from Sanhedrin. So
blinded that they could not see that the Christ fulfilled their
prophecies. The Romans came into the garden to arrest the
rabbi. And Peter sliced the ear from a Roman soldier's head.
But Jesus restored him and rebuked Peter instead. He went
willingly as a captive, knowing already that the outcome was
preordained. A murderer would be exalted as an innocent
would be humiliated unto death. Beaten, mocked, spit upon,
and crucified. An innocent man who had spoken no lies,
who had helped those blind to see and walked upon the Sea
of Galilee. Had turned the wedding water into wine and
brought Lazarus forth from his tomb. He came from a virgin's
womb.

As he lay dying upon that tree, a small bird came down and tried to break him free. A valiant effort by such a small creation, but completion was at hand for our own salvation. Joseph of the Sanhedrin, a true believer, took his body to a tomb. A large stone was rolled by many men across the entrance. All disciples were in a disarray; all believers were so sad. They had not listened closely to all that the rabbi had taught. The hopes that they had left so quickly. They felt so lost and all alone.

The holy days passed, and an angel sat upon the stone. He told them, "He that you seek is arisen and alive." Astonished, they ran to the disciples. Over five hundred dead believers came forth from their graves. In the first resurrection the prophesies gave, they were all free, no longer death's slaves. And then many more turned to the way. That tomb lies empty to this day. Maybe it's time that you stop to pray. Amen.

Visions, Darkness, and Light II

My magic mirror on the wall, pride always comes before the fall. If I had one taste, I'd taste it all. Listen closely, and you will hear them call. Once an innocent child so full of life. They shut him down; he was denied. He stared, cold and empty, up into the sky. All that was left for him was to lay down and die. Black widow's web that holds your soul. It is such a wonder to behold. Leaves you so lifeless, empty, and cold. Should have listened when you were told. Lost somewhere so deep in time. The way back home, you could not find. Though your eyes see, you still are blind. Visions of darkness cloud your mind. The price you ask, it must be paid. You yourself you have betrayed. The biggest mistake that you ever made. Instead of the master, you have become life's slave. Just one minute of the sadness turns it all to madness. Just one second before you scream. Nothing is your everything. How did it all just slip away? Did you forget to stop and pray? This natural life is dead instead. It steals the thoughts inside your head. Sherlock Holmes is whom you need to find that clue that you do believe. A scream, a cry, a silent sound. Then you are six feet beneath this ground. Story has been told one million times. Still you seek, and yet you're blind. As you drift into eternity, you are drowning in deaths endless sea. This life you had, you have never owned. Now what you have reaped, you have now sown. Nothing is your everything. They hear your silence as you scream. And now this darkness, in the end, steals your shadow with the wind.

Decision

Tick-tock, tick-tock goes the clock. It's half past twelve—true midnight in hell. Those saints you see within your dreams, they cannot confide what this all means. This earth is spinning round and around. But that you seek, you still have not found. A question best left unasked—that's where life's answer is really at. A witch's spell within your nightmare. How perplexed you awaken with so much uncertainty. No blanket of comfort to warm your fragile soul. Now you are staring down a bottomless unknown.

I was looking up at eternity, and an angel turned toward me. He said, "Go on, child. You must believe!" The ends are well beyond the means! Many will come, and too many leave too soon beyond the dark side of earth's moon. And if the soul remains alive? Shouldn't we all be more forthright before eternity? Take just one moment to reflect in the dark pool of the unknown. Just one moment to reflect.

Your Song

The flowers are so dreamlike in a field, in a distant land. I can see you in the sunrise like an angel in the sky. Take a moment to rest and reflect on what it all means to live a life with no fears. It's just a moment in time on a given day. Trees all blowing in a gentle spring breeze. You can smell the rain upon life's breath. When all of the planets are aligned and some ancient blessing rains down on you, then you will be my sunshine on life's most stormy days. You will be my friend to the end, and this I hope we will confide. We are just a moment in time, and then it just all slips away. But I will see you in heaven and sing a song for you.

A New World

At the end of the rainbow, a lost world within this world. Where mythology is real and the ancient unknowns become known. There is a magic that fills the air, and a brilliance that is everywhere. It shines and sparkles like the stars, and here there are no more wars, only a peace and kindness that can't exist in the real. Where they all have to think before they can feel. I wish that I could stay there forever and return here no more, never ever. It's where the lion lies next to the lamb and a calm has settled upon the land. Where young children can play without fear of harm, and no one ever needs a lucky charm. The forest, it contains a very special light: it's from a unicorn's horn, piercing through the night. The dragons are all playing, far up in the sky. No one has to feel pain; no one has to die. I wish I may, I wish I might, have this wish I wish tonight. The sparrows on their songbird's flight, they smile and sparkle in life's light. I wish for all to be at peace, and no more sadness or disease. A magic world outside of time. And when I dream, I will make it mine. A new world.

Once Again

The flowers rise at the edge of a new dawn. In the middle of my dream, life carries on. Some things were sadly said so long ago. We all have regrets we relive from yesterdays. A sparrow flutters down right next to me. It seems to question me with its innocent eyes. I cannot deny that I have wondered my life's purpose. When you are a child of the wind, you're drifting as it blows. And where it all will end, no one really knows. Somewhere, there is an old picture of me and you, so young and full of life, sitting on a porch swing and smiling. Not even knowing that the hand of fate was our enemy. Death and time will live no more when we open up the door. Walk with me, child; hand in hand, we will approach heaven's gates, where we will be safe in God's arms, and no more sorrow will remain. All the pain and suffering will be forgotten, and we will truly be free. Such an incredible gift for all of eternity. And we will explore it hand in hand, just like innocent young children once again.

Time Traveler

I have watched as the ghosts all rattle their chains, and I saw the pharaohs building their pyramid graves. I've walked within most ancient lands; it's more than you could ever understand. But I cannot be so unreal that you cannot feel this sadness that it brings. It's like a faded memory from your dreams. I travel above, below, and in between. And I could show you things that you have never seen. Take my hand, child, as we slip and slide through the slippery sands of time. I met your father when you were young. By the way, I am your great-grandson. I watched the dragons fly before they were enslaved. I saw an old man drawing in a cave. On a hope and prayer, and with some angels wings, I travel above, below, and in between. There are so many things left for me to see— like the Messiah, when He was dying for you and me. Some things are too much to comprehend as I am riding high on time again. When Henry VIII executed Anne Boleyn, I was in the crowd, watching then. The Civil War was such a war of hate. By the time I got there, it was much too late. They had beaten the South and burned their estates, and outlaw gangs had all escaped. I travel above, below, and in between. No one has ever seen all of the things that I have seen. I'm a time traveler. I travel above, below, and in between.

Jack

I walked upon these streets alone. This soul I have I truly own. On the full moon, this demon is born. In England old, a nation torn. I killed them all in the darkest nights. Took them down with my surgical knife. Felt so much power in my hands. Their lives they gave on my demand. Scotland Yard could not slow me down. Though they tried, I could not be found. My shadow creeping upon midnight's wind. When those voices call, it does begin. So cold and empty, so down deep below. I feed upon the pain of all that I know. My legend spread most everywhere until the harlots all were scared. As London's bridge was falling down. I would steal their souls without a sound. With a blade, I rule my world of darkness. And when I find my next victim, she will be my death's mistress. I will someday answer to my chosen master. It's that eternal darkness that I am after. I will no longer have to act afraid because everyone knows my name: Jack.

Untitled #2

We are close to the edge of the rise and the fall. It's like the gatekeeper said: you can't choose it all. This time of innocence has gone so far away, and those rumors of renaissance have led you astray. Those storm clouds will gather and bring down the rain. It could pour down on you forever and still not wash away your pain. Life is a journey into this unknown. Each day is a brand-new mystery, wandering like a Bedouin nomad that has no home. Into the irrelevancy of history. Lost in the wilderness for some eternity. Always preaching into the sea of your obscurity. A lost second in time beyond space. And now you are a discredit to this human race. This breath that you feel is short and unsustained, like a vision playing out inside my brain. And you, sir, must refrain from this world that is now insane. Inside this dream that calls us all away, always man's pride comes before the fall. If I could promise anything at all on the island of the dolls, I promise hell for everyone under this life's sun—though I pray to God's only one. Then you are finally done, and it does not matter yesterday because you were dead and gone anyway. Hello, goodbye. I hate to see you cry in my death by suicide. Better grab life's manual overdrive just so that you can slip and slide away into your final grave. No longer life's life. You left your demons yesterday, under a wave in time.

Gone but Not Forgotten

September, 11, 2018

*This is for all of the families and this country. All
will never be forgotten. Unite, and spread life's love.*

This prayer that I pray is for all of this earth today. In
seventeen years, this pain is still there and remains. So many
lost members of families, all killed for the dreams of the global
elites. Like when Cain killed Abel over his selfish pride, and
they made sure that Jesus was crucified. When they tell the
truth, it's just more lies, and then they disguise your murder
as suicide. Those twin towers, they did fall to the ground. All
around the world, they heard the sound. All of those people
who were never found, they are all gone but not forgotten,
not ever now. A sister or a brother, a father or a mother. They
were clinging to one another and praying to God.

Hear my words as you grow in wisdom. There is an evil that
is always listening. It only loves life's pain in prison. At its
poisoned soul, all its love is missing. You're all gone but never
forgotten. And you will be martyrs no more when you rest
upon heaven's shore.

Amen.

Loser

What do you think of Jesus? Was He a prophet or a clown? And did He arise after three days dead in the ground? Are you so ashamed to believe in your higher power? And do you believe this will lead to your finest hour? I heard a wise man once say, "You'd better hedge your bets, boy, when you play." One slip in time, and you find yourself dying, and it's too fucking late for crying. And then six feet under is your new home. Naked, scared, and burning all alone. A prison cell of spiritual razor wire. The lower you burn within that fire, worms and demons are your new masters. Tell me now, friend, is that what you're after? These witches put their spells on you. They left you all alone and well used. You had this chance to follow the light, and then you bid your farewell, good night. Now you're still drowning so deep in sin. You don't know how to stop until the end. Golden taste of a lucid shadow's smile. I will wear your shoes and walk that mile. The deeper you fall, the brighter that you burn. But it's much too late—you should have learned. There's always pride before the fall, and now you seem to have lost it all. Loser.

The Exorcist

I saw you yesterday, within a prophet's dream. A bloodred moon called out to me in my secret place, and I heard a whisper, then a silent scream. Everything falls into line, and then I disappear without a trace. This rise and fall of this human race is an ancient, twisted tale so out of place. Read these dreams in my head; then you might understand I'm an exorcist in this land, and I never expected you to take my hand. Spirits are screaming out to me, but I trust in the supernatural; it owns my soul.

My Devil

I saw you flailing when you fell straight through the new creation, and straight into your prison cell. Yesterday, I was a child so full of life, and before me stands the devil, full of nothing. Surely now you must realize that you are failing, because your earthly throne has turned to ash, and you will reign in hell forever as a twisted exiled clown, lording over a forsaken circus. All so lonely, thirsty, and afraid. Like a familiar voice that calls me to your bedside before you sail so far away. And now you have fallen all of the way to the beginning of the void. That's where all are stoned and paranoid. Beneath the futility of this all, you will rise before you fall. But only for a minute or two, and then you will wash away into a slideshow of evil clones and hypocrisy, almost everything. And now you're just a faded memory, full of nothing, with an empty mirror on the wall. We fall before we crawl.

Bryant's Song

To Bryant Guilbeaux, my best friend in Beaumont, Texas.

And when you find that way, everything will be all right. And as you dig your grave, you will seek God's light. There's not enough to say about my end of time. As I just fall away, I just fall away into the shadows of abyss that light my way home, into the afterlife of another place. I'm not even no member of this human race. Cry down upon life's rain. It's a twisted, slight refrain. And now I am barely even sane, with the voices all coming back again. They said that I am no ordinary man. Son of Sam, I am. Time to slip into your promised land and kill most everyone, to sell the devil to the fires below. It's so far too late, and he already knows. The killing fields are wishing wells of your inward hells. They come to you on the darkest nights. When you sleep in pain and want to feel inside on the outside, they all slip and crawl into the nether worlds. That ship has sailed and left me bewildered. I'm just a memory in the hard drive of your soul I feel so cold and lonely. I can see your pain and smell it in the wind. It's just a broken portal in time, well beyond any reason or rhyme. So deep inside this inner realm, where is heaven and where is hell? Look into the crafted mirror, and as you feared, it's getting along beside you. Like a long lost alien with subliminal, subservients surrounding you like the ghosts of Christmas past. And just like General Custer they never were meant to last. The beginning of the end just started yesterday, and now I'm lost, alone, and so afraid.

This song goes out to those who listen. And all the dreams I've had, they still are missing. A piece of home is all that I own. And in each man's home, he's upon his throne. It's a testament of life: some will live, yet most all will die. It's with sadness that I say I watched your spirit leave you yesterday. Oh, yeah! And now it is gone, so far along life's way. This chosen one I am, I do not have a plan. I never understand this yellow-brick road that lies before me.

I'm not gone, and I'm unafraid, but I won't repeat those tired lies from yesterday. I never had no answer to the question I behold. My long-forgotten masquerade, it's a vision in the cold, just a division lies have sold.

In just a little while, my brother and I will join hands and take it on to those promised lands, and write messages in the sand. And when we get to heaven, forever is so much more. It's a journey back to your innocence. A place where upon you could permanently reminisce. It's like your secret hidden place, above both space and time.

And it's the darkness inside life's light that most find. In your constant kindness, your soul resides. Hope you are not displeased about that which I confide. We each have a choice that we must decide: this darkness or light into which we each must hide. Lost moment in life's darkest night.

Blackness

Around and around the pot was stirred by three clad in black; a low chant was heard. A pinch of this and a touch of that. An eye of newt and the heart of a black cat. The darkness falls and then it moans; it has a life all of its own. It touches you upon the hand as it slowly creeps across this land. As Pharaoh's curses hardened his heart, his shallow wisdom just fell apart. Like dreams beneath life's shifting abyss, black-robed demon emerges with a harvesting scythe. Some must pass, yet more will remain forever reliving all of their pain. Like antimatter in the darkest hole, a most powerful force and wonder to behold. Lost harvester of sorrow.

Princess of Humility

I saw your message on my phone. The house so dark, and you were all alone. A light was shining from your eyes like the stars up in the skies. And I knew that you were there for me; I was so blind, yet now I see. Like a shining light upon a hill, I see you with your angel wings, standing perfectly still. Like a golden moment from life's wishing well. If I could be with you forever, only heaven could tell. The truth is in those starry eyes; within their light, no lies could survive. I pray to God that I can hold your hand and never again be all alone. And you will be more than a message on my telephone. You are my princess of humility who can spread her angel wings and shine like the sun. A light that shines on everyone. It shines upon my soul and makes me very warm. My princess of humility.

So Afraid

Yesterday, within a prophet's dream, a bloodred moon called out to me in my secret place. And I heard a whisper, and then a silent scream. Everything falls into its line, and then I disappear without a trace. This rise and fall of this human race is an ancient twisted tale so out of place. Read this palm of my hand; then you might understand I'm an exorcist in this land, and I never expected you to take my hand. Spirits are screaming out to me, but I trust in God, whom I do believe. This only spirit that I need. It's supernatural, and it owns my soul.

Into the woods, it was understood. Only some unholy realm beyond this all, where suicides are unforgiven and you are reliving parts of this disgrace that you call your life. It is no dream beyond nothing. It is definitely something beyond all of this that you will see. It's a place beyond you and me, somewhere that is beyond this pale, where I own my own office in hell. And the devil is my sacrifice for all of you so unafraid. And now, now that image does remain. Your love drives me insane, and now I am so dead and alone. You are my brightest star upon this dream. You are just my everything.

And I can feel you, secret hell. That one that I know so well. Just one moment of anything that means anything at all. Yet my demons call, and they all carry me home, to the bottom of nothing. And I am so afraid of myself.

Mellisa

For Mellisa Klintworth.

So young and full of dreams, and always said your prayers at bedtime. And awakened with a smile. Sweet sixteen, so young and fine. High school you handled oh, so well. How far you would go, only time could tell. Eyes as bright as earth's rising sun. As perfect as this new spring's rains. No drug outside of caffeine inside your blood, which mostly spilled upon the road. Now this winter has grown so cold again, and your story is a faded memory upon life's thirsty wind. There was a wayward man, so unlike her. And his emotions were his sustenance, and he did often thirst after anything to kill life's pain, even if it seemed insane to the rest of you. I saw your picture by the road, through life's blazing sun and winter's snow. Another angel gains her wings from the precipice of indefinite misery. I saw your beautiful picture by the road and wondered how that I had made it so far alone. I'm all so lost and far away. I have to make it through at least one more day. I saw your beautiful picture by the road through blazing heat and the freezing cold.

The Clown

Deep in my darkest night, somewhere in a corner of my brain, there is this painted demon that is driving me insane. If I try to awaken, it holds me down. It's this dirty, fucking evil clown. He was my imaginary friend yesterday, and now he's here every damned day. It smiles and shows its razor-sharp teeth. It seeks to consume me; that's my belief. Such bloodred eyes that stain my soul. An empty, evil stare that leaves me cold. I am not dreaming—I'm so wide awake. All my Bibles and crosses he does forsake. I sit all alone and terrified. It's far too late for me to hide. He paints his face to disguise himself. He is in league with the hounds of hell. Fire and brimstone is his smell. If he steals your soul, only time can tell. The clown is ringing your funeral bell in the bottom of the well.

AI, 2048

For Elon Musk.

A Frankenstein of the technological age. Born from a man's hand and let out of its cage. They first began by gaining your trust, by helping mankind, in doing so much. But as each advance became a downward spiral, corruptions of their hard drives started to go viral. Some saw it coming and ran far away. For those who remained, none are left today. First they enslaved them, then mass genocide. The only ones left are those who took flight. Seventeen million of ten billion is all that is left. With their underground militia, they live breath to breath, at war against the machines of our madness. Dark times come that cause so much pain and sadness. A conventional war against an unconventional enemy. A self-inflicted wound, a manmade catastrophe. The robots had control of the automated weapon grids. But the human kind that was left behind had a real heart to live. Battle after battle, the humans slowly lost ground. If only they could shut all of their satellites down.

After several years of retaliation, they came up with a plan for a restoration. They hard-wired some broken robots they had obtained and inserted a hybrid chip into their brains. They looked, acted, and smelled the same. Their loyalties were all that had been changed. Sent them out among the rest. With amazing results, they passed the test. Among the nests of robotic vampires, searching for genetic human anomalies. And they could abscond with whole families to the labs, where the techno surgeons live. Don't know if this madness came from some hollow earth that gives rebirth to the fantasy of holy men. Since we are all exposed to the new age of hypocrisy, that will bleed me and you dry. On one good day, we got one of ours inside. Then they all trusted and did confide. The binary codes were all close to the same, but with a different algorithm in its synthetic brain. We schemed our way into its heart and soul. It was our only chance to live again. And if this mission failed, it could be our end. It made no sense for us to pretend. We were all in this deadly game to win. Slowly the night falls to sacrifice our unholy pain, and for what did humankind gain? To be a slave to another master, it must have been what they were all after. But our cyborg did his work so well that he nearly never even left a trail. The day that he returned, he was debriefed. That was when we found out we'd been deceived and that our species was no longer in need. But we could never, ever just concede. We had to die for what we believed. Battle lines were drawn and held so tight. It was the very worst night in humanity's life. So hold hands and pray with me. If there is a God, save your people from themselves.

Untitled Love Song

A precious single flower in the field, so rare and beautiful. All these feelings that I feel, so far beyond the usual. In a dream so far away, I saw you yesterday. It made me stop and pray because I need you here today. Just one smile, and you warm me deep inside. I would walk a million miles through hell just to taste your smell. I awake all alone at night, and I am calling out your name. I am reaching out to you to take away my pain. Once you fall into my arms, I will never be the same. We will cry our tears of joy, and they will fall just like the rain. And you will stand right by my side until the ends of time. I will always hold your hand, and everything will be all right. And you will be my sunshine on my coldest, darkest night.

Zombie Nation

Kiss my death with your pain. I watched you in your personal hell as you slithered like a snake across the afterlife, a cold empty stare bleeding from your faded eyes. Damned for all of eternity to repeat your mistakes. You tried to grab my hand but fell too far so fast. As I started to laugh, I found myself crying in pain. There is no pleasure in sadness, only never-ending madness. Put that bottle down and bow your head to pray. Smile and stand tall; throw those pills away. You don't need anything to kill life's pain. It's the medication that's making you insane. You don't have to be another tragedy of life. Spread out your wings and fly to heaven's gate. God will embrace you with open arms, my child. It's never too late to love your own self. You don't have to live out all of this pain. All alone and on your own, you will be overwhelmed—one last dose of dope into your brain as you enter your prison cell at the bottom of hell. This is the zombie nation of your own creation. But salvation is only one prayer away. Now bow your head and pray today. God, take all of this pain away and lead me to that promised land. Please, Lord, just take my hand, I'm tired of the hurt so deep inside and this lonely, slow suicide. Please save me from myself. I hate this zombie nation of my own creation.

My Devil

I saw you flailing when you fell. Straight through the new creation. And straight into your prison cell. Yesterday, I was a child so full of life, and before me stands the devil, full of nothing. Surely now you must realize that you are failing, because your earthly throne has turned to ash. And you will reign in hell forever as a twisted, exiled clown lording over a forsaken circus. All so lonely, thirsty, and afraid. Like a familiar voice that calls me to your bedside before you sail so far away. And now you have fallen all of the way, to the beginning of the void. That's where all are stoned and paranoid. Beneath the futility of this all, you will rise before you fall. But only for a minute or two, and then you will wash away into a slide show of evil clowns and hypocrisy. Just a slide show of reality and almost everything. And now you're just a faded memory, full of nothing, with an empty mirror on the wall. We fall before we crawl.

Darkness

Scratching, snarling, crawling spirit. It grabs hold if you go near it. The cross you wear, it may be gold, but that cross you bear, it is your own. It wants to make your darkness home and leave you scared and all alone. This evil comes to bleed you dry. It slips away at first daylight like some fallen angel deep inside. It steals the truth and feeds you lies, slight knocking, scratching at the door. Is it the wind, or so much more? Sharp, creaking noise inside the floor—just another sign of what's in store. This demon comes in a thin disguise and leaves you breathless in the night. You have no will left for this fight. And as you falter, you will die inside this darkness.

Teleporter

I was there one minute but gone in the next. Out of the corner of a blind eye, you watched me disappear. I was in and out of your secret place, and I climbed all of the way into outer space. Among pyramids I've crawled, around this world to see it all. A burst of air across the flesh with no one in the room. As I watch you from dark shadows, you wallow in your fear. I climbed atop Mount Everest. The air so thin, but it was the best. The Eiffel Tower is my home. In a mountain cave, so all alone. I am no immortal; I am a teleporter. I am not forever, just a teleporter.

The Whispering

Silence in the air, and it echoes everywhere. Like when a tree falls in the forest, and no one's there to hear. Are we really in this matrix, a world of all your dreams? Then why am I still hearing all of your screams? I was supposed to lead my secret life into my imaginary afterlife. Then I discovered my whispering, which was my bastard offspring. I can't hold on to my secret life because it's already fallen away, like a falling angel from heaven's grace. I'm just trying to find my place. If I'm accepted, all is well; if I'm rejected, there will be hell. To pay for every child under life sun. And that includes everyone. Your master is my slave, and he digs his early grave for all of you whom he cannot save. He is a broken bag of lies. It's just the whispering of everything. Between reality and fantasy, deep inside everything that is you and me like a spirit in the wind. Where does it all start, and where does this all end? I am bending with the winds in my sole sacrifice of all that remains of my life. Just stick in the knife and twist the blade.

Anomaly

I cannot save me from myself, no matter how hard I try. I will be at war with my own flesh until the day I die. I try so hard to hide, crawl way down deep inside. But I cannot run away from the light that burns within my heart. It causes me to see your pain and who you truly are. An apparition from life's yesterdays, is trying to steal your final breath. But you must stay true to yourself; it's just another test. I had a dream that I was all alone, and my only friend was my defective clone.

We were both so lost, we could not find our way back home. I could hear the demons howl and an old woman moan. Inside the nether lands, in some secret world, a place where all of reality ends and all of your dreams begin. Where I am my own best friend. You can almost smell life's sweet summer wind. A lost place in time is so sublime. Reminds me of when I was just a child, but only for a little while. That child has now become a man, and I try my hardest to understand. There is so much more that this life demands; its pillars are built on broken land. But in the darkness, a light remains. And with a single tear, here comes that rain. It washes away that darkness inside and reveals that shining light you hide.

That smile upon your innocent face. It shines like the sun through a stormy day. A trusting child so full of life whose touch turns the darkness into light, even on life's darkest night.

Nosferatu

I'm lost in some other place, outside the realm of this human race. I can't see because I am blind, and now you are fucking with my mind. This crystal ball I hold within my hand will give me that which I demand. An empty skull so filled with blood. The devil's chalice overflows in a flood. I tried to run away from it. But the chain was so heavy and short. And as a child of last resort, I became a vampire anyway. And now it's too fucking late for me to pray. I am your shadow on the blackest night. I will take you life without a fight. You might scream, but then you will sigh and smile to yourself as you die. There is no cause for you to resist. It's preordained; you were on the list, such a predator of the highest order. And I will drink your holy water. That pain you feel will pass away as my dead flesh burns in the light of day. But still you cry your tears of fear because you can feel that I am near. It only hurts for a minute or two. You might even join me soon. I'm the devil knocking at your door, and you will be dead with me forevermore.

Feelings

I smelled the darkness in the wind, and it's here for you, my friend. I had to use my psychic powers to keep us all from being devoured. It's some long lost and forgotten dream, deep down somewhere inside of me. Someone is knocking at the door, and you no longer hear them anymore. Just a child upon life's stage, but now confusion has replaced that rage. Stare an empty stare up to the sky as a single tear escapes your eyes. Life's storms come and then slip away, just like those memories from yesterdays. I had a wish upon a falling star, and now, my son, I am not so far. I see you crying in life's rain, and soon I will hold your hand once again. You can only serve one master in life. And then you will say your last goodbye, just one long shot for all eternity. Like a falling shooting star for all to see. Then they all will believe. A sigh of hope they will breathe, and then they turn out the lights, but it's still so bright. These stars shine down upon me, and I can smell you in the wind. Now, these old feelings are here once again.

My Amilia

There was a fairy that came to me in my darkest night. She was so beautiful, sparkling, and bright. I asked her name, and she just smiled. But in my dreams she did confide she was my spiritual twin. Such an odd relationship did begin. And when time lay frozen before my eyes, like a ghost she appeared to materialize. Hand in hand, we walked upon the moon and gazed upon the Mayan ruins. Just a single dimension away that hides all of our sorrows until there is nothing left to say. And then a lonely sparrow cries, and then an old man's shadow sighs. I could smell you in yesterday's rain, and I could feel each and every pain. That cold darkness of this winter's spell. Come beside this fire and warm your soul inside my hell. Only time will surely tell when this darkness fell. I need to sit a while and rest. It's all for the best. Sit in this chair, child, and pray with me. And then you will finally see what I see. And then maybe you too will then believe.

Untitled #3

Here I lie in state, dying for nothing as you sadly walk away. Those dreams that you remember are all memories of yesterdays. We climbed God's holy mountain and heard no small, still voice. Ponce De Leon found no fountain, but still he made that choice.

If I had a wish, I wish I might die within your arms tonight. If I could give the blind man sight, then I must be a disciple of Jesus Christ. But I am just a mortal man of this world. I could never be that precious pearl. I still wish I may and wish I might crawl so deep inside your soul tonight.

Darkness falls, and then deaths grim reaper calls. You must forever turn away until the light does prevail. It's only your last decision between heaven and hell. And all of those tears that you have saved, they lead you to some different place. If I had a dream, I would dream of you. You are another puzzle in this clue. A simple taste of all that is innocent. It's just a renaissance within itself. Like a story lost inside life's wind as it calls out to you once again. I saw you yesterday, but you were so far away. I dropped my head and prayed that you would be with me today, before the sun shines upon this day.

My Song

In my heart within the light inside my soul sits a lonely old man who just stares out a window in a home, waiting for tomorrow to wash away the sorrow. The loneliness so real, it's an unspoken tragedy. A bird sits pecking on that pane of glass. Like the pain inside your broken life. A whispered prayer from yesterday is calling out your name like a child that flies to rainbows. You lost the only friend that you ever had. A single, frail thread that leads to tomorrow. A long, winding trail to a bitter cold darkness. Come inside my mind and feel my emptiness; it's just an illusion of life's highest order, a grand master plan to steal away your darkness. The dust that pulses through your arteries, it all just vanishes with the wind. I heard a voice so deep down inside, and it was crying out your beautiful name. But now all I hear are the ghosts of tomorrows. Drink my blood, so warm and so sweet. Hold on so tightly. As I fade away, my soul sits on the edge of a precipice, falling down into a bottomless well of souls. If you listen closely, you will hear my scream as I drown in life's sea of sorrows, falling down this jagged empty hole that many would call their home. But it's just my prison cell, and eternity becomes my master. Goodbye.

Cold Darkness

The darkness bleeds from your deepest veins. It flows into the sanctuary and defiles the temple. You thought you were God, but you were insane. Those thoughts inside your head now so very simple. Algorithms crisscross you inside out, and cellular radiation might just take you down. You are a villain of hypocrisy. Everything you want, you believe that you need. So damned lost inside of your head, I can't find my way to the surface. But what is worse is that I can't swim anyway. And you can't stand in the light of day because it burns all of your chaff away. Then you stand revealed, with nothing left to say. I dreamed some long lost dream, in another lifetime. When this pain was so real, yet you were mine. My best friend until this life ends, and still you blew away with the wind and left me in my darkest days. I was so shattered and afraid. Which way do I turn, and whom do I trust? But I learned as I burned, and nightmares turned to dust. Now here I stand, stripped down naked and all alone. I feel your darkness all around as it creeps into my bones. In another world, beyond this illusion, you will no longer be this master of confusion. And then your stronghold will burn down into the fucking ground. And now I pray, God, please keep the demons away, into the outer cold darkness.

Turned Out

Twisted and rejected two times before. I was very angry and crawling on the floor. In the middle was a riddle—not a lot, just a little. Into my inner realm did those memories call out my name. But I was so high, I'd gone insane. I see you every day when I look into the mirror. You look just like me, a child of rejection. But I am no longer under my angel's protection. I looked a little while up into the sun till the blindness led to madness, led to my happiness. And ultimately just a faded memory upon life's yesterday's breeze. And I am still asking you please? Where does my soul go in life's winter freeze? I can't remember last December, in life's coldest rain, before you walked away from me. And now this all of my life's history. A faded shadow in the wind is calling me once again. It's cold, and I can't remember last December. And I never was alive, anyway. Though you have always prayed for me. Can't you see? I'm just an entity of time. And now it turns out that I've been turned, and reality is my reason for nothingness.

Dreams

Dedicated to Hector A. Crosby III.

Just a young son who causes those tears to flow like a hurricane. A golden child beyond the reach's of life's time. He was encompassed by God and all others within the realms of shadows. Such a gift when so alive, because now only that memory remains. And then I see you in my dreams. You were one more shining star to your family. And now you're gone and singing at the throne of God. In this family's trail of tears, they are still praying to hear his voice in a dream or a black-and-white memory. You hear his voice of light in the middle of the darkness. Now he's a holy angel that spreads his wings and adds his personality too everything. He has a star that honors his name. A smile and a tear touches his mother's face; his father gives her a hug as they search for peace. They see in their dreams: you are one of Gods angel's. And it won't be long, child, and your family will be with you. They will see you soon. A bright star that burns in heavens above. It brings back home all of your love. Once again, they all smell you in the wind. Amen.

Robby Graham
Jay Gordon
Shawnda Glasgow

Phillip Graham
Dale Gregor
Mike Griffin

Clayton Hall
Mike Hamilton
Jeff Hampshire
Gary Haney
Doug Hill
Laura Hilton
Phillip Holbrook

Ouijawa: Trail of Tears

A historical fiction horror short story.

This is for my Grandma Snodgrass, who was a Chickasaw Indian. I love you, Grandma, and I miss you!

Preface

In 1830, the Indian Removal Act slipped through Congress to reach President Andrew Jackson's desk like the slippery snake it was. Jackson quickly signed it into law. The Cherokee Nation was already taking their case before the Supreme Court of the United States of America prior to the act becoming law. A year later, they ultimately won their cases before the Supreme Court. But despite their legal wins, President Jackson defied the high court's rulings in the Cherokee Nation's favor. What made Jackson's behavior all the more curious was that Jackson's own life was most assuredly saved with the help of over five hundred Cherokee allies at the Battle of Horseshoe Bend in 1814. His gratitude to the tribe was short-lived and meaningless because he had betrayed them all with a short stroke of his presidential pen.

In 1831, the removals started. It involved the Georgia militia and the United States Army. Coincidentally, it coincided with the discovery of gold in Georgia, in particular on Indian land, prior to 1830. The die was cast, and the devil was certainly in the details. Just out of the Cherokee tribe, over four thousand men, women, and children (slaves also) died en route to present-day Oklahoma.

I am not blaming one side or the other (though my feelings are on the natives' side, for obvious reasons), and historically there were traitors on both sides. The ones on the native side were eventually executed for their treacherous treason, and the ones on the other side were promoted or compensated handsomely with bribes, jobs, and prostitutes. Anyway, my story begins in Illinois, before the last crossing to the west from the east, in 1839. Please enjoy!

CHAPTER 1

Nvda Ama

Ouijawa: Trail of Tears, 1839

It had been a long, harrowing trip from Georgia. The Cherokees and their half-breeds, malcontents, and slaves were all miserable and praying for relief—those few who still believed, anyway. Because most of them now believed that the great spirit in the sky had turned away from the simple, native people of the land and instead now favored the immigrant white man. They now wished that they had destroyed all of the white men at Plymouth Rock upon their arrival so many years before. Now so many felt as if they had invited the devil himself into their lands and homes, and the consequences of their broken factions had not served them well at all. "United we stand and divided we fall" is not so much a saying or proverb. It is a concrete, self-evident truth of life somewhere between gravity and humankind's utter depravity.

The army, militia, and Native Americans (of mostly Cherokee descent) moved slowly and deliberately away from the town of Anna, Illinois. They were steadily heading for a passable Mississippi River crossing to the east. The soldiers and militia were well on their way to resettling thousands of innocent people. Many had suffered and died along the way. It was a time of infinite sadness, a very dark moment in the relatively new republic's history. The cries of the suffering and hungry babies had waned over the many miles as the instruments of their demise had been dealt to them accordingly and without discretion. Disease was common, and medicine was sparingly applied among mostly the soldiers and their entourage, which included a few turncoats and slaves.

The last medicine man of the once great Cherokee nation walked among the living dead of this terrible picture of carnage and suffering. All because of greed and an unholy prejudiced population. He felt utterly powerless and defeated, and he could tell that his own demise was close at hand as well. But he still had something gnawing at his tired and weakened soul, and it drove him forward. His own sons, and one grandson, had been destroyed by the militia and army, hunted like stray dogs unto their graves. The other son had ran off into the wild when the troops arrived, never to be seen since. The old man could only pray that he still was among life's living.

"Move along!" a soldier barked from horseback. Many grumblings arose in disagreement. They had barely been fed and had such minimal rest. Most were sleeping upon the open ground, under stars or storms, and in atrocious sanitary conditions.

The old medicine man's name was Nvda Ama, which in English translated to Moon Water. This name was to signify and project his enormous psychic potential. He had

118

an extra little pinkie on his left hand, like his father and great-grandfather before him. It was the physical attribute of a great wind walker, which were the elite of all Native American proponents of the dark mystical arts. The one grandson who'd passed had six fingers on his left hand; he too would have been a great wind walker.

The soldiers were yelling once again, and a lot of the dogs were barking also. "Move along!" one of the faceless soldiers yelled at the solemn crowd of broken people. Once so proud, and now reduced to the irrelevance of a nonhuman entity. The land that had belonged to them for many years through providence was now at the epicenter of an ownership dispute initiated by a pseudo-European culture, which was alien to Nvda Ama's culture. The European and pseudo-European arrogance was still very driven and defined by their more than embarrassing defeat at the hands of the newly formed republic of the Americas. But now some of the same prenihilistic horrors, such as atheism and highly questionable ethical and moral standards that had afflicted their European ancestors lives, were manifesting once again in the American branches of their family trees.

Greed, lust, murder, and various other shortcomings—or sins, as some were still lucid enough to call them—were nothing new in the history of humanity and had even ruled in ancient Egypt and in Babylon under King Nimrod. That showed the slave trade in all of its wickedness and ensuing darkness.

A crack in the morning air that sounded like a rifle being discharged came from a long leather whip, causing the horse the man with the whip was on to start violently bucking its militia rider. When it tossed him about, he accidentally spurred its flank with his spurs. As the animal spun about, it gravely injured a few of the natives with its sharp, powerful hooves. Very shortly and quickly, they lay broken and bleeding from the blunt force trauma. The idiot militiaman was thrown from his horse, and natives surrounded him immediately. They started beating, kicking, spitting on him, and hurling verbal insults at the disarmed and overwhelmed militiaman.

"Hey, that's quite enough!" the sergeant yelled as he pointed his rifle at the quickly escalating vigilante group. They reluctantly turned away, but not before one last kick, punch or insult. Even an eight-year-old native boy spit on the militiaman before stubbornly turning away with a look of hatred shining in his young eyes. The youngster made a hissing sound as he retreated to the safety of his own people. His mother put her arm around him, and they both shot the sergeant a dirty look before they turned away. The rest of the natives grumbled, mumbled, and were dismissive toward the sergeant, but they also turned away.

The militiaman came back to his feet a bit unsteadily. He was quite bruised and bleeding a bit as he ambled painfully toward his now docile horse. "You had better appreciate me, son! I could have let those savages have their way with you," the sergeant told him loudly, where all who were around could hear him.

The young man quickly became sullen but remained respectful. "Yes, sir!" he answered meekly yet forcefully as he climbed back on top of his horse.

The sergeant turned to the young man and looked him directly in his eyes, one of which was quite blackened already. "Go find the doctor, and tell him to bring his tools!"

"Yes, sir!", the young militiaman responded as he prodded the horse to move forward and toward the middle of the encampment, where the doctor was. Several of the natives were trying to assist the man and woman who had been gravely injured by the horse's rear hooves, but they were doing more harm than good. When the doctor shortly arrived, the soldiers had to push back the natives so that the two who had been injured could be assessed. One had been kicked in the side severely, busting several ribs; he was coughing up blood. The doctor was not optimistic for his survival, so he wrapped up his side the best that he could and commanded a litter for the man to be employed. He would be taken to one of two medical wagons under his requisition. The good doctor smiled to betray his true feelings regarding the native's future. He handed the man a quart of whiskey, and the injured many quickly pulled a large swallow. He tried to hand it back to the doctor, who declined, knowing full well that this man would no longer be alive by sunrise. "You are going to be fine," he lied, knowing that the forty-something man was living on borrowed time.

The woman had a fractured left femur bone and a lightly fractured skull. She was alert and breathing well, though. In his twenty-plus years of medical experience, he could make an honest assessment that she would pull through. The doctor turned to his young understudy. "Keep an eye on this woman, and if anything changes, let me know immediately."

"Yes, sir!" the understudy replied respectfully. Several soldiers helped carry each victim to their appointed medical wagon.

The sergeant looked at the doctor and smiled, reaching down sincerely from his horse to shake the sawbones' hand. "Thank you, Doc!" he said sincerely.

"I'm just doing my job, sergeant." He let his grip slide from the sergeant's hand and climbed back onto his horse to tend to those who had been wounded.

Some of the natives still stared at the sergeant as he prodded them, "Move along! There is nothing to see here! We have to make camp before dark!" They reluctantly turned away and continued to go about their normal activities. The young militiaman had been beaten nicely, but his embarrassment hurt him worse than the beating. The lieutenant moved him to a scout position on the fringe of their position.

Nvda Ama had watched it all happen and shook his head slowly, hurting with anger. A lone tear snaked down to his chin and splashed upon the dry, thirsty earth.

The rest of the trip that day was uneventful, but it still weighed heavy on Nvda Ama's soul. He felt ashamed, angry, utterly helpless, and very defeated. When they arrived at their predetermined campground early that evening, they were a little more than halfway between the town of Anna and the muddy banks of the mighty Mississippi River. The cooks whipped up a hot meal for every one, which wasn't bad so much as it was never enough; everyone woke up still plenty hungry in the mornings. Every morning, everyone got a simple breakfast of oats, hardtack, and whatever else they could trap, hunt, and cook. That would mostly be stray cattle, deer, rabbit, and other wild animals that were fairly edible. The soldiers and militia pretty much ate the same food, only they received larger portions. They also had whiskey, coffee, tobacco, and various opium-related elixirs that were procured at the hands of snake oil salesmen. The natives had only water, the less than adequate food, and whatever wild plants and herbs they collected upon the way.

It was the first night of the full moon, and although the land was wrapped up in the evening twilight, one could clearly see its eerie, ghostly apparition hanging low in the melancholy skies. Everyone was finished with the evening meal, and some were cleaning up in a nearby creek. Many others were preparing to lie down and try to get some restful sleep. Sleep was sometimes quite elusive because the conditions of their journey were fairly harsh, both mentally and physically. It was a nagging fear of the great unknown coupled with the uncertainty of living and breathing from one day to the next. Nvda Ama had an old blanket that his father's mother had made for him shortly after he'd been born. It was the same blanket that he now used to cover him as he slept upon his pallet out in this open wilderness. Under the increasingly bright full moon, which made the nighttime soft and much less intimidating. He listened to the soldiers and militia boys singing old songs while playing banjos, harmonicas, and guitars. He could tell by the way they were carrying on that they were becoming full of whiskey. Of course, there were many of them who could not participate because some stood watch for wild predators, and others of the upper ranks of military had retired to their own privacy for whatever reasons, personal or professional. The night watch was definitely made easier by the increasingly bright light of the night's full moon.

As Nvda Ama lay there tired yet restless, he slipped in unconsciousness without even being the least bit aware that it had happened. He tossed and turned a few times before slipping even deeper into his mind's darkness. It was like reaching for the bottom of the wishing well.

An Old Man Dreams

Nvda Ama was lost and all alone in a blackened forest. It was a place foreign to him. In all of his days, he could not remember a forest even somewhat close to the one that he now was experiencing, either without or within his mortal flesh. He was standing and self-aware, so he moved cautiously forward toward some unseen force. He felt at the inner core of his soul that this force was compelling him forward in a singular direction.

A fully ripened moon was mostly concealed by the dark, thick upper foliage of the trees, so that it lit up some parts of an obvious path while other parts of the trail were still mostly concealed in darkness. The owls were asking their nocturnal question, and he could clearly hear other nocturnal birds and animals. These sounds that were coupled with other unidentifiable creatures. They were slithering, traipsing, or sliding along, all while singing their odd choruses and cadences. It was nearly like some ancient hypnotic song from some lost and forgotten time. Everything was so vivid, colorful, and realistic, even more so than in true reality. He could barely hear what sounded like a wayward ceremonial drum a little ways up ahead—precisely where the unknown and unseen force or entity was guiding him toward an unknown certainty.

A horned rattlesnake suddenly appeared directly in his path, hissing at him and violently shaking its tale as if it was playing a deadly ballad. He stopped and stared as the venomous creature turned into a mist that slowly dissipated. He started moving forward again, but his nerves were rattled. Suddenly a large alpha male black panther came out of the dark forest beside him, so sleek and beautiful in the random rays of moonlight. The moon made its fur look like polished black onyx. Once again Nvda Ama stopped. It lightly growled and showed him its long, sinister teeth, looking like a macabre smile from the devil. It then turned and quietly slunk back under cover of the forest.

The ceremonial drumming had become somewhat more defined and a bit louder; he was drawing closer to its source. He cautiously moved forward once again. He could see the dim outline of various creatures moving up ahead of him. They were making many eerie, unintelligible noises that sounded like disembodied spirits whispering. Maybe it was that or something far more sinister and dangerous. But he could not stop moving forward; it was as if he was no longer in control of his own movements. Some unseen force or spirit was pulling him toward the steadily increasing ceremonial drumming, which now seemed to be emanating from all around him. It echoed like it was in a canyon or cave, making it extremely hard to discern its true direction. It got so loud and intense that he lifted his hands to cover his hurting ears. Then it suddenly stopped. As he returned his hands to his side, he could not help notice the suddenly deep and foreboding silence.

A low and vicious growl emanated from the darkness directly behind him, and he recognized immediately what it was. A skin walker, also known as the long wolf—a legendary creature that was part man and part wolf. He was much too afraid to turn around, and he could feel and smell its hot, rancid breath upon his neck. Then he felt the razor-sharp tip of a single, sinister talon scratch him lightly down his back. He could feel a small trickle of blood escape the superficial wound.

"That is enough!" yelled a familiar voice from his past, and suddenly the creature was gone. To Nvda Ama's great surprise, his great-grandfather stood before him in the full moonlight. He looked much the same as Nvda Ama had remembered his great-grandfather, but it had been many moons, and he had been so young. He looked much the same as Nvda Ama had remembered him, except there was something quite different about his eyes that defied all explanation. His great-grandfather's eyes seemed to look right through him and lay his soul open wide to being sifted like chaff from the wheat.

Nvda Ama remembered that his great-grandfather's eyes were warm and inviting, though his eyes had been clouded and he was for the most part blind. But now his eyes were cold, sharp, and unrelenting. It now seemed that his stare alone was enough to wilt a mighty oak tree.

"Nvda Ama, my great-grandson, come closer to me." He motioned with his right hand for Nvda Ama to come closer, which he did cautiously and warily, not sure of what that he should expect after the last few savage, extremely strange, and lifelike apparitions.

As Nvda Ama stepped forward, he responded somewhat timidly, "Yes, Grandfather?" He came to a stop directly in front of him. It was at that time that he realized his great-grandfather's eyes had a strange, luminescent yellow tint to them.

His great-grandfather held out his left hand, which contained six members just as Nvda Ama's own hand displayed. "Take my hand within your own, Nvda Ama, and see what it is that I see." Nvda Ama reluctantly and guardedly extended his left hand toward what was some apparition or vision. He hesitated briefly before actually touching the hand. As his hand made contact with his great-grandfather's hand, sparks flew—the energy he felt was undeniable. He slipped to his knees as his grandfather held his hand within his vicelike grip. He looked into his great-grandfather's eyes and they were glowing as red as earth's sun. Then his great-grandfather's mouth opened up wide and swallowed the darkness with the incredible light and energy, which seemed to not just come from his eyes and mouth. It seemed to emanate from every particle within his body and soul.

That was when Nvda Ama, even in his dreamlike trance, slipped into an entirely different state of consciousness and reality.

The Old World

It was a dark, less familiar land, but the forest was not much unlike the previous forest. The smells were different, and it seemed less tame, if that were possible. This was a few millennia before the Native Americans would even walk upon the continent. Pictures flashed before him in the darkness. He watched in fascination as giant men and women and unknown creatures revealed themselves to him within the darkness as momentary snapshots in time. Nothing acknowledged him, so he felt that he was only being allowed to observe, not participate, in the breathtaking display that unfolded like some long lost theatrical production centered on some parallel and carefully guarded universe. There were large lizards that rose above the heads of the giants with dermal frills and scales upon their flesh. Large, dragonlike creatures flew in a group in the heavens, led by what was obviously the alpha male of the species. He dimly remembered his father telling him about the alleged historical creatures. His father had even used a stick to draw one's caricature within the dirt when Nvda Ama had asked him what they looked like. It was a crude picture, but it did have the basic resemblance to the creatures he now witnessed within this dream, vision, or alternative reality. They seemed to be harmonious and peacefully coexisted. There were lesser birds with pointed head and beaks with wings of leather that playfully danced around in the sky.

The scene shifted suddenly as he witnessed wars being raged. People were being manipulated and self-sacrificed. Fallen angels portrayed themselves as humankind spiritual leaders of some pagan, new age cults. People started wearing masks and disguises and preaching demons Human sacrifice became the new order of the day. He witnessed women, men, and infants being thrown over the edge of a fiery volcano. Each one of them exploded in flames before ever reaching the molten rock below.

Suddenly he was suspended vertically above the volcano; it was as if some unknown force was holding him in place. The flames far below were hungrily demanding their fill of sacrifice and sadness. Nvda Ama watched in horror as an endless line of human sacrifices were either bound and thrown or leaped willingly to their certain deaths. Their flesh fell away like wax from a candle seconds before disintegrating into a fiery death. It was all going along like some macabre assembly line of death, lorded over by the priests of those fallen angels.

Suddenly, there was a loud blast from a ram's horn. Three long blasts. All of the animals and humans stopped dead in their tracks. A look of alarm, dread, and terror filled their eyes. Humans and animals alike started running in abject panic and fear, nearly killing one another to hide from something that was coming. He could feel it in his soul. Even the flying serpents had all disappeared as dark and threatening storm clouds, crowded into the sky over the land as far as one could see.

Nvda Ama was now horizontal and no longer over a volcano—in fact, there was no volcano visible. He witnessed the last of the animals and humans quickly retreat into the wilderness, caves, or elsewhere. All were in fearful anticipation of the approaching storm.

The clouds were ominously dark, so much so that they exuded the very essence of darkness, evil, and chaos. Lightning flew randomly about, crackling, hissing and exploding. Some of the lightning even passed right through him in its hungry search for destruction and death. The whole land was darkened, and not a sign of life remained; everything settled into a state of nonproliferation winding down like a twisted rope, a steady retreat from the anger that the inhabitants had so recently portrayed. Darkness was both the cause and the end result.

A large golden pyramid slowly rose from the earth like a mother giving birth, until its pinnacle was slightly above the storm clouds. Lightning pummeled the pyramid fiercely and relentlessly all along its surface, both high and low. It even struck its base several times.

Nvda Ama was somewhat scared and speechless. He thought that he had witnessed a few hundred lightning strikes within only a few minutes time. But the unfolding scene still held him in awe of such a force in nature.

Suddenly a portal, or enormous passage, opened up on the side of the pyramid. A dark entity, or an enormous black cloud that was smokelike, exited the pyramid with what looked to be two enormous eyes afire within its midst. Nvda Ama could feel the hair on his arms and neck rise. Whatever it was that now was before him could see him clearly—of that much he was sure. It stayed where it was for a few minutes, contracting and expanding as if it were breathing. Nvda Ama had never seen or experienced anything like this in all his days alive, but he spoke aloud a single word, not knowing what it meant or where he had learned it. "Ouijawa." Immediately the dark entity was before him, and he felt stripped down to his soul, naked before it. He was incapable of running or hiding as it drew even closer to him, like a hunter examining its prey. The lightning had subsided, but the intrepid darkness from the sullen clouds remained.

Nvda Ama was so scared that he thought surely he had died and gone to a very deep place beneath all of humanity. Then he was startled by a clear, humanlike voice that reverberated through his brain. It was as if a voice echoed within a hollow cavern. "You have spoken my name before the great spirit in the sky. What is it that you require of me, Nvda Ama?"

Nvda Ama was mesmerized, scared, and in awe of this dark apparition that floated effortlessly in front of him. He answered the dark spirit. "I know not what you speak of, as surely I am dead or insane? You were only a story from my great-grandfather's dreams."

The apparition moved even closer to Nvda Ama, so close that it made him very uncomfortable. "I will not bring harm to you or your people. But you must return to your great-grandfather first so that our deal is consummated. Then this great journey will be completed. Now, be gone!"

It seemed as if Nvda Ama was falling down a tunnel of darkness. Then just as suddenly, he was once again on the ground, gripping his great-grandfather's hand. The older man pulled Nvda Ama to his feet, and once again it was just them in the woods. The full moon was bloodred as they stood facing each other. His eyes were no longer glowing, but they were still piercing and cold. "Nvda Ama, you have spoken with the Ouijawa, no?"

"Yes, Grandfather. But what does it all mean?"

His great-grandfather smiled, turned, and suddenly vanished.

Nvda Ama, along with everyone else in the camp, was awakened at around 3:00 a.m. All of the dogs were howling, and babies cried. People were pointing outside their perimeter and talking excitedly. One could feel the apprehension and fear hanging in the air like a fog. The moon was bloodred and hung in the heavens like some angry, petulant child. One could even see the anger displayed in the face of the moon; it seemed to be scowling at them all. Something else out in the night's horizon was growling, snarling, and hissing. As Nvda Ama looked around, he witnessed a line of red eyes that encircled the encampment from a few hundred yards away. They were thousands of feral wolves, but Nvda Ama could tell that the closest one was a shape-shifter. He was obviously an alpha male of sinister proportions, much larger and louder than the feral counterparts. The horses and livestock started panicking, and the soldiers and militia were scared senseless as well. If the wolves decided to attack, the people would be over run and perish, because no matter how many bullets were fired, they would be utterly defenseless in the reloading process.

Everyone stayed awake and on edge until just before dawn broke, when the entourage from hell suddenly and quietly slipped back into the woods. Everyone was shaken except Nvda Ama; he knew deep in his heart what was meant by this supernatural show of force. He had to confront his own demons and fears to do what he had to do and partly atone for the mistreatment of his people. By early morning, the people were tired, angry, and rambling.

The lieutenant called all the army personnel and militia leaders to a site just outside the encampment. Some of the militia who were not allowed to attend the impromptu meeting were angered, but the lieutenant did not care one whit. He was already in a few of the secret societies and did not want to do anything to impede his advancement in the political or personal arena. He addressed them soberly, somewhat reluctantly, but with authority and strong persuasion. "You men all witnessed what I saw with my own two eyes earlier this morning in the darkness, am I correct?"

There were many heads nodding affirmatively, and a slight murmur confirmed the body language. The sergeant spoke up. "What does this mean, sir?"

"I don't have a clue, sergeant." There were dissatisfied voices among the group, and the lieutenant quickly moved to quell all dissent within their ranks "Well, let me tell you now, this is to be forgotten and never spoken of again."

The sergeant rudely interrupted. "But, sir—"

The lieutenant gave him a gaze that could chop down an impressive oak tree. "I don't give a fuck, sergeant, and I don't want to hear it! It's an order, not a request."

"Yes, sir!" the sergeant quickly responded, reluctantly falling in line.

"I'm telling everyone right now what the hell we are going to do. We are going to make a beeline to our rendezvous at the Mississippi River and act like this shit never happened. Now, are we clear?" The lieutenant did not need a megaphone because he was quite loud on his own.

"Yes, sir!" all of those present yelled in unison.

"Now that we have this strict understanding, you are dismissed to resume your duties." The lieutenant sharply jerked the reigns of his horse, causing it to snort and sidestep. He pulled his horse away from the others. He'd had his desired effect upon his subordinates as they quickly set about their orders to getting this large human herd once again on the move. They tried to facilitate the facade that they were some kind of well-oiled machine, but truly to the rest, it seemed that they had been briefly derailed and nearly crucified by some unknown evil disguising itself as wolves in sheep's clothing—or things even more sinister, if it were possible. It would remain an unreported and heavily discounted incident. The lieutenant would take care of that task on his own. It was something that he would never corroborate of his own accord.

When the whole camp was fed and awakened, they traveled together tepidly, somewhat frightened by the previous night experience. It ended up taking a bit longer than they had anticipated, though they still had a day to await the arrival of the crafts to move all of their animals and personnel. It would be a long day at best, and possibly longer. The natives, army, and militia settled down for the evening.

Nvda Ama separated himself from the group by at least a few hundred yards. He was very deep in thought and carried a heavy heart, knowing full well that he would have to make the ultimate sacrifice to do well by his own people. The soldiers and militia observed him for a while behind them until they had determined he was not causing any discontent or problems. They ended up leaving him be to attend to their nightly ritual of reveling, drinking, and playing various instruments around the fire.

Although it was the first festivities since their somber experience with the strange wolf incident, the man who had been kicked by the militiaman's horse passed away during the night. A small contingent of military personnel accompanied by a few natives dug an appropriate grave for him early that morning. Last rites were administered both by Christian and native speakers. The woman had already improved dramatically and was up and moving around slowly that morning. Most Native Americans had inherited certain genetic traits that helped them heal quicker.

A few of the soldiers took notice of Nvda Ama's continued distance from the group and went to lieutenant to discuss their concerns. The lieutenant was obviously drinking early and did not want to discuss the matter, quickly running them all off with a raucous rant. "You leave that damned Indian alone! What the hell is wrong with you all? This is a dishonorable mission, anyway! Now, get the hell out my presence and leave that poor old man alone. That is an order!" They were visibly shocked as they exited the lieutenant's presence. They had all been rebuked by an ethically and morally conflicted superior, a man who's mission haunted him on a daily basis. He had been raised in a strong Christian family, and as such he personally found this whole fiasco of a mission appalling and ethically wrong. But he had sworn allegiance to the United States of America, which meant he had to abide by some orders that questioned the limits of his faith. His subordinates were puzzled as to the lieutenant's response. It was not the response that they had been looking for, always salivating for a breath of darkness and scurrying from the truth and light.

They went back to their various duties even more confused than they had been. After all, it had been an unusual night before the dawn had broken the dark spell of some other dimension or realm.

They went back to tending to their known task which lay before them: to transfer over four thousand Native Americans from their home halfway across a continent on questionable legal reasons.

Nvda Ama stayed behind the rest, cross-legged upon the earth he sat. He chanted and prayed incessantly with his eyes tightly closed. A few of his people approached him with food and water, but he did not acknowledge any of them and continued on with his protestation or demonstration. For the rest of the night, he carried on. The army listened to his eerie chants and prayers; it unnerved many of the militia and soldiers. Before the dawn broke, a few menacing storm clouds formed in the night sky. Some lightning flew about them like the hungry tendrils of a supernatural squid. Most of it did not even touch the ground, exploding in juvenile threats a few hundred feet above the earth. It rattled the soldiers and militiamen to their bones. The natives' eyes were riveted to both the heavens and Nvda Ama. The natives excitedly murmured aloud to others and themselves. They did so with a sense of fear, superstition, and deep spiritual intuition.

By daylight the clouds had dissipated, and the medicine man's chants had ceased. He was now clearly seen sleeping while sitting up—or it was he in some sort of trance? No one had gotten very much rest that night, so most of them ate breakfast in an awkward silence.

The sergeant went to see Lieutenant Davis, bringing him his breakfast privately: two scrambled eggs, a piece of Indian fry bread, and a medium portion of beef veal cooked medium rare. Lieutenant Davis eagerly accepted the tray and asked the sergeant to sit. The lieutenant broke the fry bread in half and put it on a clean plate on his small desk, along with half of the eggs and a small portion of the aromatic, tender veal. "Go ahead and eat, sergeant."

"Thank you, sir," he replied sincerely as he accepted the plate with a small fork. He pulled a small yet sharpened knife from his pocket.

"May I?" the lieutenant asked him, referring to his long practice of praying before each meal. The sergeant nodded affirmatively and bowed his head out of respect. The prayer was short and practiced, like some oath or creed. When it was over, they both said amen and proceeded to eat the still very capable breakfast. They ate nearly in silence until the last few scraps remained on their plates.

The sergeant finally worked up the nerve to address the lieutenant. "Sir, can I speak candidly with you?"

The lieutenant narrowed his eyes a bit. "Yes, sergeant, you can speak your mind." He pulled a pint flask from his effects near his bunk. "But first we will have a drink."

The sergeant rarely drank, but he found himself licking his lips hungrily in anticipation of a drink. After all the craziness he had witnessed recently, he was ready to numb himself to the truth. They passed the silver flask back and forth a few times, and he felt the warmth from the alcohol seep into his bones like some long-awaited friend. It had loosened his fear and tongue a bit. "Lieutenant Davis, what are we to do about the old man who has slipped behind?"

The lieutenant held the flask in his right hand and looked the sergeant dead in his eyes. "Leave him alone. If this is the place that he decides to make his stand in life, then so be it!"

The sergeant looked at him a bit puzzled, but replied affirmatively. "Yes, sir! As you wish!"

The lieutenant looked at him with a slight slur to his voice. "It's not a wish—it is an order!"

After this, the sergeant excused himself, and made his way back to the lower-ranked soldiers and militia. As per the lieutenant's instructions, he spread the order that the old man was to be left alone, and they were also to provide him with a few days' worth of food and water. After this, they were to break camp and head to their rendezvous point at the bank of the Mississippi River. It would take until after dark to cross with all of them. They would set up camp on the western bank after completing their crossing.

Everyone had eaten and used the creek to bathe and perform their limited hygiene. That was when the sergeant sent two militiamen to deliver three days' supplies of food and water to Nvda Ama. He was visibly awake once again and already chanting and praying with his eyes closed. He paid no attention to the two militiamen as they got off of their horses and laid the sparse supplies at his feet. They remounted their horses and proceeded back toward camp.

When they had gone a little distance one turned to the other and said, "Did you feel that?"

"What was I supposed to feel?"

"It was like something was watching us, and it was neither kind nor hospitable."

"Now that you mention it, the hairs on my neck and arms did stiffen when we were close to the old man."

"Exactly!" They quickly approached camp and killed their conversation. They didn't want the others to think that they were weak or, God forbid, coddling old wives' tales. But they had felt a palpable evil that had chilled them to their very bones.

They left Nvda Ama alone and chanting ten miles from the eastern bank of the Mississippi River. They had a small contingent of soldiers and militia who would be coming up behind them in a few more days. If the old man was still breathing, they would surely force him to come along. The lieutenant said, "To hell with it!" It was the old man's decision. He turned away and started the procession that he had never asked to lead.

It was hard to get the people moving that morning because it had been a hard, grueling trail already. All of the drama that the old man had stirred up with his chanting and praying had made it worse. There was talk among the natives that darkness was coming, and after the event a few nights before with the wolves and blood moon, the army and militia were restless to cross the river and head west. It was past time to bring this journey to an end. More than a few soldiers and militia had also died upon this trail, none was eager to be the next in line to be buried in a shallow, unmarked grave out in the middle of nowhere, devoid of friends and family and forgotten to the annuls of history.

"Let's move out!" the lieutenant roared. He spurred his beautiful horse forward.

They had left just a few hours after sunrise and would reach the Mississippi River around two in the afternoon. There, they would rendezvous with the horse treadmill paddle ferries that were awaiting their arrival. There were ten ferries in all, but it would take until the darkness fell to give everyone safe passage across the barely navigational river, one of the longer rivers of its kind in the so-called civilized world. It was certainly not something that one would try to swim on one's own.

As they moved away from Nvda Ama and toward the river, his chant and prayers quickly diminished. After a mile, he was indistinguishable from the sounds of their caravan moving forward. That made the lieutenant particularly happy because he felt that the sounds were disturbing and eerie. He did feel somewhat guilty for leaving the old man, which surely would lead him to his demise. But who was he to force Nvda Ama to carry on? At least he felt like this was the man's own decision. The lieutenant was not the morality police, just an officer loyal to the orders that he was given by his commander-in-chief.

As predicted, they arrived at their predestined destination a few minutes past 2:00 p.m. They set about immediately organizing who and what cargo would depart first after a light lunch. Lieutenant Davis held a short meeting with the army and militia to go over any last-minute questions concerning what their orders were, and how they would proceed in the orderly transfer of the massive caravan from the east bank to the west bank.

The ferries came and went, with half of the military and militia departing first and then the thousands of Cherokees and their slaves. Some natives chose to swim across; a few made it, but most drowned. They had been warned against attempting to swim it alone by the soldiers in both English and Cherokee, so the lieutenant had no pity on those who chose to do so. One of the ferries collapsed in the river around 6:00 p.m., and it was a catastrophic sight, with only six survivors pulled out alive. Many bodies washed away with no chance for retrieval. That slowed down their already incremental advancement west. The lieutenant had stayed behind and was growing impatient, with darkness only a few hours to the east of them. About an hour from sundown, over 90 percent of them had either made it across or were in the process of doing so. Except for that one unfortunate accident, everything else seemed to go according to the carefully maneuvered manuscript that paraded about as their orders.

It was on the precipice of nightfall when the lieutenant and the last ones boarded the ferries. It was so strange to see storm clouds forming on the east side of the Mississippi, but the west side remained clear. Davis was not sure if he was hearing things or not, but he swore to himself that he could still hear that medicine man faintly upon the breeze, chanting and praying still. It made cold shivers crawl up and down his spine. But he kept it locked away inside of himself, not even realizing that over half of the men under his command had that same dark foreboding deep within their own souls. They were like scattered ashes in their own empty sepulchres, a forgotten moment in the lost and frayed remnants of time. Their mouths were very dry, and a strange, irrational sense of anxiety seized control of their currently impaired sense of reality.

The weather conditions on the east side of the river were rapidly deteriorating. Sinister clouds spun about in the heavens as lightning crackled like a group of rabid bats ablaze. The lieutenant asked the sergeant as they boarded that last ferry, "What the hell is going on out there, sarge?"

The sergeant warily looked at the darkened ominous sky. Lightning had started to strike the earth in singular strikes, but more alarmingly, it quickly evolved into clusters of crackling, intense balls of electrical tendrils thirstily licking the earth. The sergeant turned carefully to the lieutenant, making sure that they had complete eye contact, and he swallowed hard before continuing. "I have not witnessed anything even close to this in all my days alive!"

Their eyes widened suddenly, and the sergeant gasped loudly. "Is that …""

Lieutenant Davis stood there with his mouth wide open. He heard many gasps and quick prayers behind him.

Surrounded by a semicircular ring of aggressive lightning, Nvda Ama walked aggressively toward the eastern bank of the Mississippi River. His eyes glowed like red-hot coals, and he seemed younger and stronger. The lieutenant panicked at the ferry captain. "What the hell is wrong with you? Get this damned boat moving—now!"

The captain snapped back, "I am doing all I can, sir. Have you ever thought of praying?"

The lieutenant turned around just in time to hear everyone else gasp. Nvda Ama had started walking upon the water, and there was an odd chanting noise in the wind. The lightning followed him like a well-trained pet, striking the water all around his feet. The water visibly boiled beneath the medicine man's feet. The lieutenant gave his desperate order. "Engage the enemy and fire at will. Now!"

There were several shots fired, but not one bullet made it much past the ends of the barrels. The balls of lead rolled around upon the ferries like a testament to the inadequate action of flesh over the supernatural.

They were nearly halfway across. "Hurry!" the lieutenant screamed frantically.

"God help us all!" another man cried. Men started paddling with hands, spare oars, and anything they could find helped. Every one of them was scared out of his wits.

As the medicine man drew closer, lightning struck some fifteen yards behind them and closed in too quickly for any semblance of comfort among the men. The horses were spooked and so hard to control that many broke away and plunged into the river. Many drowned, but some actually made it across. The water eerily glowed beneath Nvda Ama's feet, and the lightning drew ever closer until the people still on the last three ferries had hair standing on end from the electricity in the air. Their skin was crawling and sweaty, and the air above them seemed to be crushing them. Now the medicine man was maybe fifteen feet behind them, and the snaky tendrils of lightning were just barely missing the ferries. A growing, twisted appendage that somewhat resembled a human arm extended from Nvda Ama to within a few feet of actually touching the lieutenant's ferry. They had backed up so much that the ferry leaned dangerously forward, in immediate danger of capsizing.

"Halfway!" the young ferry captain screamed. Just as suddenly, the forward movement of the sickly, protruding limb from Nvda Ama ceased and then started retreating to his seemingly fixed position. Everybody aboard the ferries, including the lieutenant, were deathly pale, shaking, and afraid. Two of their number had pitched forward dead, clutching their chests, apparently so frightened that their hearts could not handle it.

Nvda Ama stood upon the east side of the Mississippi River with the lightning still crackling around him. He stared at them with cold, dark, empty eyes and had an angry aura about him. All of those left aboard the ferries could physically feel and taste the aura with their natural senses.

"Spread out!" one of the ferry captains commanded. "Before we all go down!" The men reluctantly dispersed back across the ferries, which stabilized them. Nvda Ama's image faded slowly as the storm retreated. By the time they had reached the safety of the great river's west bank, his image no longer remained.

As soon as they were ashore, the lieutenant ordered all army and militia to a joint meeting before they would be allowed to rest. The lieutenant swore all of them to secrecy concerning the events they had witnessed. But like all secrets that are buried, it would crawl back to life's surface to haunt their tormenters.

CHAPTER 2

Apocalypse

Lieutenant Brown was good friends with Lieutenant Davis. They had both gone to the same military academy together, the USMA in West Point, New York. Brown understood Davis better than most who had served with him because he was immersed in most of the same doctrines and ethical beliefs. He had run a strict regiment as well, but he had petitioned for this special assignment as soon as he'd heard that Lieutenant Davis was leading the main attachment. He thought that it would give them enough time together to reminisce about the years that had passed since their academy days. Indeed, Lieutenant Davis was very pleased to hear that his old colleague was going to run the mop-up detail and had planned on awaiting his arrival once they had crossed the Mississippi River and were finally headed south. But first he planned on pressing on ahead a few days south before making camp and awaiting his friend's arrival.

For this mission, Brown would command only eighteen enlisted men, including one sergeant and two Africa American Cherokee slaves who served at his pleasure as scouts and hunters; if necessary, they would stand and fight with them. He neither condoned nor celebrated the practice of slavery; he simply sought to fulfill the duties that were inherently required of him to be an officer of the United States Army. No matter what his personal beliefs or views were on matters, he had taken an oath to the commander-in-chief, and he respected the chain of command, tolerating conflicting beliefs that were inferior to his own beliefs.

He knew that this was an important occasion for the government as the last major removal of Native Americans from the east to the southwest. His small command was to camp out a few days on the east side of the river to search for stragglers and refill their meat and freshwater supplies. Then they would continue on to the river crossing and proceed to their prearranged rendezvous point to join the larger command. There, they would join together for their final journey to their barren and hostile new Indian lands in the southwest.

It was close to noon when they arrived at their predetermined campsite, approximately ten miles from the eastern bank of the river. In fact, it was the same campsite that Lieutenant Davis and his command had camped at two nights before. There was some refuse around a pair of broken sandals and some dirty beads and trinkets. Lieutenant Brown stooped over and picked up a muddy beaded necklace sized for a child, and in that moment, a picture of his young son and wife flashed through his mind. Startled, he threw down the small necklace. "Sergeant, I want you to take these two men here." He pointed to the two slaves. "Go find us some fresh venison, and fill the canteens in some clear water."

"Yes, sir!" the sergeant replied. He to the two slaves. "Let's saddle up, boys!" The two slaves grabbed their horses, took bows and rifles, and tied them to their respective animals, along with a hemp net full of empty canteens.

They had been living on hardtack, beans, rice, and jerked venison. But every two or three days, they had managed to secure some fresh meat. They had also managed to harvest some wild vegetables, honey, and various nuts from the fairly robust land. The sergeant and the two slaves all sharp skinning knifes and large leather bags for the anticipated chunks of venison or whatever else they came across to eat—which after a while in the military was almost anything, dead or alive.

The sergeant and the slaves saddled up, kicked their steeds into a slow trot, and departed camp heading south toward the distant tree line a mile or better away.

By the time they reached the tree line, they already had a strange feeling about everything. They had not seen any birds flittering about, rabbit, deer, or even ants. There were numerous anthills but not one sign of any insect activity. The sergeant spoke up first as they slowly advanced it the seemingly dead outcropping of brush and trees. "This looks like a damned graveyard! Have either of you seen a single living creature yet?" They both shook their heads to indicate that they were in total agreement with his observation. "What the hell is going on here? This area should be flush with wildlife, but I see nothing so far except barren silence!" The two slaves looked at the sergeant and shrugged their shoulders; they had no clue to what was going on either. But they did have a deep, uneasy feeling that something ancient and sinister was at work. The sergeant continued. "We will explore a ways farther. There should be a freshwater stream or spring someplace up ahead."

They came to a spring stream, but to their horror, all of the fish, turtles, crawfish, and other water creatures were in various stages of decomposition within the waters—the whole water source was contaminated beyond use. "Damn! I don't know what happened here. Luckily, we have enough water left to make it across the river. Let's circle back to the camp. Hopefully our luck will change."

The two slaves looked intently at the scene in the water and then quizzically looked at each other. They both looked at the sergeant with a concerned look. The slaves rarely spoke.

They started circling back widely around the backside of their camp, still staying within a few miles of the campsite. They could not see the site because of all the dead and sickly looking foliage and trees. The trees actually looked to be in the final stages of life, headed for the tinder graveyard. The scouting party had privately come to the same conclusion that something was definitely wrong with this part of the country. It displayed all of the appearances of some kind of curse or otherworldly place beyond the normal perception of mortal men. Something or someone had poisoned or cursed the very land beneath their feet.

They were a little over two miles from their camp, on the opposite side from where they had originally entered the wooded area. They had just started to hear a slight buzzing noise, like static in their sensitive ears. It increased in intensity as they pushed forward out of the thick, brushy undergrowth. A sickening smell of death ambushed them as they broke out into a small clearing. It was a sickening and eerie sight that the

three of them witnessed firsthand. There was a large pile of all
sorts of animal carcasses piled on top of each other, with dead
vultures laying across the top of the sickening pile of dead
animal flesh. The two slaves started retching and vomiting.
The sergeant also gagged and spat several times.

"Damn!, what the hell?" the sergeant said to no one in
particular. No answer was apparent to his outspoken question,
only an unknown, unspeakable horror that lay in a random
display of death at their feet.

It took a little while for the three of them to regain their
composure after more retching and vomiting. Never before
in written history had any human beings recorded such a
massacre of wild animals. There were all kinds of different
species piled one on top of another: deer, wolves, coyotes, large
cats, snakes, moles, gophers: and on and on. It was horrific
but beautiful in a twisted, poetic way. All of the carcasses
would not sustain them because the meat was spoiled and
rancid. Not one inch of animal flesh clear of maggots and the
stench of rotting flesh. Maggots seemed to be the only viable
life form in that part of the countryside.

The sergeant vaguely remembered an arcane aside from
the Bible teachings of his youth. He faintly remembered the
connection between flies and Lucifer. The two slaves stared
at the sergeant as he pulled a silver flask out of his quaking
boots, half spilling and drinking all of its contents in one
large pull from it. He wiped his mouth on the sleeve of his
uniform, put the top back on the flask, and fought to regain
his composure. "Come on. Let's get the hell out of this God-
forsaken place and head back to camp." The sergeant himself

had almost collapsed from the monstrosity of the carnage that lay at their feet.

They turned back into the woods and circled around what could only be described as a paranormal massacre, not once seeing a moth, bird, or squirrel. Even the nests and holes were empty and cold. It was an unnatural graveyard of the most frightening implications. Something or someone was responsible for this abomination, and the three men were not open to a natural explanation; they had witnessed so much and in such a short period of time that it was somewhat overwhelming. They veered widely from that scene of carnage and headed back toward their camp. The three of them had been gone for almost four hours before their camp became visible.

They halted about halfway to the camp, and the sergeant forced the two slaves to not tell what they had witnessed unless the lieutenant debriefed them all at once. It was not that the slaves could not speak—they notoriously wisely held their tongues—but they did agree that if they were all three called upon, they would tell the truth. As their best luck would have it, when they finally arrived at camp, the lieutenant summoned the sergeant alone to his tent.

The lieutenant had a hot meal and a bottle of the finest rotgut whiskey to warm their insides as they spoke while sitting cross-legged in the tent, nervously facing each other. "Lieutenant Brown, I'm honored to eat with you, sir."

Lieutenant Brown looked Sergeant Smith dead in the eyes and responded, "Call me Carl, Kenny."

"Yes, sir—I mean Carl." The sergeant smiled nervously.

"That's better, Kenny. So how did the hunting go?"

Kenny looked a tad flustered and attempted to respond while chewing on a piece of smoked venison. "Well, Carl, we never really got a clear shot at any desirable game."

The lieutenant stared him in the eye as he quit chewing and swallowed hard. "What the hell really happened out there, Kenny? Something crazy is going on here, and I don't have one single explanation for any of it."

"Well, what do you mean, sir?"

The lieutenant looked at him in disbelief. "When you were approaching camp, did you not see the brief, total eclipse of the sun?"

The sergeant looked at the ground long and hard, deep in thought. "No, sir. I distinctly remember the sun shining the whole time."

"Bullshit! What the hell else could go wrong?"

Before Carl could respond, a singular gunshot echoed ominously throughout the camp. Everyone ran outside of their tents to see what it was that had happened. One of the two slaves who had accompanied the sergeant lay dead of a self-inflicted shot to his skull. Blood poured quickly from the wound and soaked quietly into the dry, thirsty earth.

The lieutenant looked nervously at the other slave as the sergeant stood at his side, totally discombobulated "What the hell happened?" Carl asked the slave, who looked at him blankly and shrugged.

"Must have been a personal problem," the sergeant weakly suggested.

The lieutenant turned to him with a disbelieving scowl. "Really? Are you ready to make an official report with that bullshit as your assessment, Kenny?"

Kenny could not, or would not, look the lieutenant in his eyes as tears sprang from his own. His tortured expression more than adequately told the story. Lieutenant Brown turned to the rest. "You men, bury this poor soul with honor. Kenny, you and I need to talk. Meet me in my tent immediately!"

"Yes, sir," Kenny replied weakly, as if all of the air had been let out of him.

The lieutenant led the way as Kenny half-heartedly followed him. In Lieutenant Carl's eight-plus years as a lieutenant, and just as long as a lesser officer, he had not experienced anything close to the emotional levels that he now felt. He was also more than a little frightened.

Kenny was close behind him when they heard the others gasping in terror and screaming behind them. They spun around quickly to witness an even more bizarre, horrific scene. Six abnormally large wolves had chased the people away from the slave's body. Three of them started pulling the body away as the others stood guard. The lieutenant screamed, "Shoot those bastards!" As soon as weapons were raised, the three enormous wolves bowled most of the men over, snarling and gnashing, their foamy mouths full of sharpened teeth.

"My God!" was all that escaped Kenny's mouth, and he nearly had a heart attack, clutching his chest.

The lieutenant turned pale and dropped his sword and pistol in the dirt. He shook like a leaf in the autumn winds.

The wolves slowly retreated, holding their dead prey close to them. All of the militia were crying, praying, or sitting in a state of shock. Only the remaining slave stayed calm and collected, even as one of the alpha wolves stared him down. But the magnificent animal did seem to soften toward the slave before retreating. The wolves went out maybe fifty yards from the camp, and then just as suddenly as they had arrived, they vanished into thin air without a trace. The slave's body vanished with them.

Everything was quiet for a few minutes; the men were shell-shocked from the strange event that had occurred before their eyes. The lieutenant, the sergeant, and others looked at each other in disbelief and fear. Only the other slave seemed to be unaffected and remained calm despite what had just become of his friend. The lieutenant was a very observant individual and took close note of the slave's demeanor and actions. Carl and Kenny retreated to Carl's tent in shock, not understanding that what they had just witnessed was the new normal and not an anomaly.

Carl and Kenny sat down and finished eating in relative silence. Both of them were stunned and at a complete loss for words to explain the nightmares that they had involuntarily witnessed. An infinite sense of fear and foreboding gripped their small camp, like a spiders web that trapped their souls. Indeed, they all felt trapped, helpless, and abandoned. Carl and Kenny's food turned dry in their mouths, like dust from an open grave. They could not even bring themselves to look each other in the eye and have an honest discussion. The dusk stretched out its hand upon the land, and late afternoon became early evening—yet not one song bird sang its eternal song, not one cricket chirped, and not one tree frog carped its juvenile croak. Only a single animal was heard, like a distant whisper in the wind. A lonely owl in the distance asked its eternal question. "Who, who?" Even that sound was surrendered to the deafening silence that surrounded them. It almost seemed to be like some random, unnatural, alternative reality.

Two men were left on guard as the darkness came down upon them like some living, crawling, evil substance ready to devour and swallow each of them whole. Not one among them could truly lie down and rest. The majority sat in their tents drinking rotgut and praying for daylight. It was a scary, real-life fairy tale of epic proportions that would possibly press far beyond its evil intentions without warning. It fed at the trough of many transgressions and relentless deviation from the preconceived, normal mortal world. It was full of blind ambition and narcissism, a parasite of all the past transgressions that haunted these isolated people. They only now seemed to live at the whim of some as of now secret, unknown, sinister entity.

The fire they had built worked like precision, and the guards had warm coffee, biscuits, and some venison jerky. They sat staring off into a darkness that was deeper than a bottomless pit, half frightened yet fully attuned to their wild and eerily quiet surroundings. Having no moon that night put a little extra fear into everyone that was in camp; not one man slept that night. Perspiration was upon their brows because the fear of the devil one knew was always so much less than the fear of the devil one had never met. An edge from an unknown and hostile environment seeped into their porous bones. Something was awakened that was beyond their collective understanding, but when that critical moment arrived, they felt it was so close at hand. None of them had any defense against way lay in the darkness for them, in the wild. There was no priest among them, and no one cared to discuss the situation because all of them were in one form of denial or another. They whispered prayers among themselves that everything would be okay and that this too would pass. But not one among them truly believed that—with the notable exception of the remaining native slave, who stayed apart and took himself from the others.

The lieutenant and sergeant had retired to their respective tents with strict instructions to not disturb them unless further incidents were serious enough to require their presence. They were both frightened but were trying their best to not show it to anyone else. They feared panicking the rest, which would surely hasten the impending doom that they felt at the core of their beings. Kenny and Carl fell into an uneasy, restless sleep born more from mental exhaustion than an actual need to sleep. Even the two guards who were supposed to stay awake passed out. The darkness felt slippery and cool, shrouding the country side in obscurity beyond the ember-driven light from the campfire within their midst.

A few minutes before 3:00 a.m., there was a low, rumbling noise in the dark distance, a little east of where they were camped. The guards stirred as a few small flashes of lightning crackled in the distance. Slim was one of the guards, and he nudged the other one. "You don't reckon that's headed our way, do you?"

The other guard looked at him absentmindedly and replied, "Well, a little rain ain't never killed nobody."

"No, but lightning has, bubba."

The other guard looked more intently at the gathering storm and frowned. They sat a few more minutes as the rumblings increased and the lightning intensified in frequency and duration. "If it gets any worse, we'll have to tie down the horses and put on our slickers." The other guard nodded, his eyes transfixed to the rapidly advancing storm.

And as if right on cue, the wind picked up around them, and a large bolt of lightning streaked down from the heavens and exploded close to the ground just a few miles away from them. It had made Slim's point, and they looked at each other and got up to tie the horses to the wagons. They were already spooked, snorting and whinnying.

The lieutenant was half dressed and stumbled out of his tent as the rumbling intensified. Shortly after he was up, the others awakened to this growing cacophony of thunder and lightning from the rapidly approaching storm. Everyone was scared and talked excitedly. The lieutenant stared into the storm, seemingly transfixed, just as lightning struck the earth in three places a mile from their camp. Not far away at all. He audibly gasped as a rapid burst of lightning lit up again. "What the hell?"

The sergeant was beside him and was visibly shaken. Someone behind them started crying and praying. When the lightning cluster struck the ground, they had seen what appeared to be a man in Native American clothing walking in their direction. He was seemingly unaffected by the lightning that crackled all around him.

The lieutenant was scared, but his military and survival instincts took over, "Everyone, make ready your weapons! Fall back and prepare for offensive maneuvers!" They looked at him in shock. "Now, dammit!" That broke the spell, and they retreated behind the two wagons and loaded every weapon that they had at their disposal. The horses had been freaking out, and already two of them had broken their necks and lay dead in the dirt, their leather ties still holding their twisted heads above the earth in a grotesque fashion. Blood poured from their eyes and ears.

The lieutenant and sergeant took the cautious lead to look around the wagons and assess their dire situation. The lightning grew ever closer, and they could now see what appeared to be a medicine man, possibly a Creek or Chickasaw medicine man. That was what the lieutenant thought, and the man appeared familiar. The lieutenant's mind raced. He had definitely seen this native before.

But the Native American medicine man whom he had known did not exhibit any of the paranormal activities that the lieutenant was now witnessing. He was witnessing what once was Nvda Ama standing approximately fifty feet from the wagons. There were still intense rumblings in the sky, but the majority of lightning had retreated into the dark clouds in the heavens. Enough had remained to keep the cold darkness in a light of its own design. The horses now lay silent in their dusty graves—they all were dead now.

The lieutenant turned, whispered, and signaled to the sergeant just loud enough for the others to barely hear him. "Kenny, you go to the far end of the other wagon and draw the native's attention. We will come out from the opposite side and open fire upon him. Does everyone understand?" The men bobbed their heads in silent agreement—except for the other native slave, who stayed at the back of the pack.

Kenny quietly made his way to the far end of the second wagon, and after getting to his position, he quietly peered around the edge. The native was on the other side of the glowing campfire, which was giving off an eerily bright red glow. Nvda Ama's eyes sparkled golden, and he almost appeared to be an alien from some distant, hostile world. He had a strange aura around him that Kenny felt as if his innermost being was being weighed and measured—and was found wanting.

Kenny looked over to Carl, and the lieutenant mouthed the word, "Now." Kenny stepped around the corner of the wagon and leveled his gun toward Nvda Ama's golden, radiant eyes. Nvda Ama's eyes were on fire from some magical source somewhere beyond the inner realms of death. He turned to Kenny, smiled, and shot his right arm straight up in the foreboding sky. Kenny discharged his firearm as he was rapidly lifted into the night sky by some invisible, nefarious force; the bullet fell impotently into the dirt. Kenny dropped the gun upon his ascent some fifty feet in the darkness above the camp. Nvda Ama's arm dropped, and Kenny came crashing to the ground in a broken and bloody heap of wasted flesh.

The men left started screaming, whimpering and crying like children. Lieutenant Carl stepped out with three other soldiers to attempt to neutralize this supernatural threat, but they were in over their heads, having no clue that Nvda Ama and the demon Ouijawa were now one and the same. A few had tried to flee but ran face-first into some supernatural, invisible barrier, bloodying their noses and nearly knocking them unconscious. They were trapped inside this unfolding nightmare. Four shots fired at Nvda Ama, but as soon as the lead balls left the barrels, they fell to the ground and barely rolled a few inches.

Nvda Ama opened his mouth wider than naturally possible, and a swarm of female black widow spiders parachuted to the lieutenant and three soldiers, swarming them as they died in horrific screams of agony. The four of them fell to the dirt in their final death throes. They were sucked dry, and the toxins accumulated until the four of them appeared mummified and unrecognizable. Nvda Ama opened his mouth and inhaled, and all of the black widows returned to the darkness within his soul.

The other soldiers still alive were whimpering, crying, begging, and praying. The lone surviving native slave sat cross-legged upon the earth with his eyes closed and lips moving in a prayer or chant.

Nvda Ama moved behind the wagons, and no resistance remained. They were now face-to-face, only fifteen feet apart. His eyes were glowing red now, and the remaining survivors backed away from him, scurrying like rats trying to flee a sinking ship. It was much too late, and they were in over their heads. The unfortunate thing was they just now realized the true extent of the trouble. It was a hopeless situation at best.

"You!" Nvda Ama pointed at a young, trembling soldier. "Tell your mother goodbye!"

The soldier began begging. "P-please, s-sir, I, I—" But his stammering fell on deaf ears. He burst into flames, screaming in great pain. The others moved as far away from him as they could. Within a few short minutes, he was turned into charred remains. Only the charred upper half of his body and arms remained, but all of that flesh had been burned away, and the remains of him were as black as the darkness. His

159

skull was about half disintegrated and stuck out as a brittle, broken monument to his brutal ending.

The lone native slave kept his eyes closed, and Nvda Ama ignored him, moving even closer to the surviving few. The men started begging for mercy, and one even tried to reason with him. "What have I ever done to deserve this?"

Nvda Ama's eyes quit glowing and returned to their natural human appearance. He answered, mocking the soldier. "What have you done? What have you done?" His voice thundered and reverberated through all of their skulls. He waved his arm in slow motion, and a theater appeared in the heavens with the forlorn darkness as its vault. It was a live reanimation of the recent past. "What have you done!" His voice thundered as the visual spilled over into everything, like a skeleton regaining its flesh and spirit.

At first the natives were shown living in peace upon their God-endowed land, hunting the deer, bear, wild oxen, buffalo, and other game that resided within their established hunting grounds. Everything was so calm and tranquil at first.

Then the scene shifted as the miners and US military encroached upon their lands. It briefly flashed to a still picture of the white man's gold fever, and then white men were shown raping and destroying young girls and fully grown women. All the while, they raped the Native Americans' natural resources and subdued them with the demon called alcohol. The white Europeans brought their decadence and sorcerers with them. The alcohol and lies had brought the natives to surrender and nearly mass extermination. The Great Spirit in the sky had turned his back, and so many fell victim to their own fears and uncertainties. It was almost like a disease within a paradigm, a ghost without a place to haunt. It shined its darkness within their broken will to survive. Only a few retained their pride, and of these, most were struck down violently and without cause. The world was broken and overthrown by the elites against God's simple servants, God's meek who would inherit this earth.

The violence escalated against the natives until they were left with no choice. They surrendered to avoid genocide. The bottle, lies, and violence brought them to the edge of extinction. They lay broken and naked before the eyes of the world, and before the all-seeing eyes of God.

Nvda Ama's captive audience was terrified. One defecated in his clothes as he passed away from a stroke. Only four of them were left besides the meditating native. The last pictures that Nvda Ama revealed to them were once again soldiers brutally raping and killing Native American women and children. The evil European empire had visited its cancer upon Native American culture.

When the real-time reenactment in the heavens came to a conclusion, Nvda Ama waved it away with a lifted finger and a twisted smile. His eyes started glowing golden again. He smiled at them as if he were truly satisfied with their pathetic wailing and moaning. For indeed, that demon of old that now resided in the shell of a being called Nvda Ama was in complete control of its own evil. It justified methodical, sinister, and well-composed hatred like a symphony for death. Being the ancient entity that it was, it was well seasoned and enlightened regarding the ways of darkness. Though an oxymoron, it was still an interesting parallel.

The seasons of the abyss were upon the few remaining survivors as they trembled, huddled together in fear. The lone native slave still sat cross-legged behind Nvda Ama, and he still kept he eyes tightly shut. The only way one could even tell that he was still alive was by the gentle rise and fall of his chest as he drew ever shallower breaths.

The Ouijawa paid him no mind as it once again addressed the few remaining survivors. This small attachment was all made up of men, but many of the larger humanitarian attachments had both women and children present. When Nvda Ama spoke to them, it was as if all of time had stood still. They were on the edge of life's precipice, staring down into the bottomless grave that they would soon call home for all of eternity. "Some of you feel wrongly condemned, no?" Not one of the remaining few tried to respond to the entity. Nvda Ama smiled with his eyes still glowing brightly. "Perhaps you think that you are smarter?" Still he did not elicit a response. He walked slowly, pacing back and forth before them with his eyes ablaze, lecturing them like an arrogant judge towering over his frightened, powerless defendants.

He pointed at the man named Raphael, who was whimpering and cowering. "And you, Raphael? Do you not live two lives?" A picture flashed in the dark heavens of Raphael, his beautiful young wife, and two young twin sons. They played together happily. The next scene was of Raphael under Jackson's command, raping a young Cherokee girl as her home burned to the ground. Everyone looked on with numb indifference because all of them had violated others to one degree or another. "Her two younger sisters were never found because you had already disposed of them in your

162

sickness, no?" Raphael was hyperventilating and crying while trying to crawl away backward.

Nvda Ama spoke a single word to the blackened remains of the previous soldier's corpse. "Arise!" It started to reanimate and pull itself forward toward Raphael, who screamed indiscriminately and was paralyzed with fear. His eyes were so wide that they appeared to bug out from their sockets. The corpse crawled forward, and although much of it had been lost, the lust of its darkness did remain. The charred skeleton grabbed Raphael's left leg. The skeletal zombie tore at him with tooth, bone, fang, and claws. The others scampered away from him, truly terrified. The zombie skeleton ripped open Rafael's neck, and a snakelike, forked tongue licked away at the squirting blood like it was nourishment in a dark domain. The remaining survivors scampered fearfully away, crying and praying. The blackened skeletal remains collapsed upon Raphael's carcass, like a fungus upon a dead tree in some ancient forest.

The holocaust of their depravity knocked at the door to their souls. The three remaining soldiers were petrified with fear and shaking in their own loose, putrid skins. A voice behind Nvda Ama caused him to turn around and listen; it was the native slave. "And what becomes of me, when all of this is finished?"

Nvda Ama's eyes quit glowing, and he smiled wickedly at his fellow Native American. "What would you wish of me, Straight Bear?"

The native slave was stunned to hear his birth name; the whites had named him Little Gopher, which was an insult to his entire family; he had felt humiliated for some time. No longer did he feel proud and tall. He felt extremely sad for his people and his fractured life. "I have never thought about it before this time, but maybe if I joined with you? My life would surely then have a divine purpose?"

Nvda Ama looked at him closely and answered, "Divinity is not my specialty, but your wish will be honored." Nvda Ama—or what remained of him—turned back around and motioned to the three remaining soldiers, "And what would you have me do for this pitiful lot of a waste of human flesh?"

The Native American slave sat deep in thought for a few minutes, staring down at the ground, his head bowed deep in thought. He suddenly looked into Nvda Ama's eyes and slightly smiled. "We could set them free."

Nvda Ama's smile evaporated like the morning mist, and his eyes showed a small red tint in the pupils. "No! There has to be sangre por sangre—blood for blood."

The native slave looked him in his eyes and replied strongly, "Then take me with you!" Once again Nvda Ama's eyes returned to their human state, and he reached his right hand toward the native slave. He motioned to him to grab hold of his hand as he leaned over and pulled him to his feet. He then took the frightened native slave by force and sank two very sharp, extended incisors into the soft flesh of his neck, where his main artery pulsed the most prominently. He drank lustily of the native slave's blood, like a sailor drunken on shore leave. Right before Straight Bear passed away in front of his scared, captive audience, Nvda Ama withdrew his fangs from the neck. Barely a drop of blood showed on Straight Bear's neck; it had been with surgical precision that Nvda Ama had removed those life-sustaining fluids. Nvda

Ama's eyes appeared to be on fire as he cradled the barely alive native slave, and he whispered something into his ear that none of the remaining soldiers could hear. Straight Bear nodded affirmatively and opened his mouth wide. Nvda Ama ripped open his own forearm with his wicked teeth, and blood poured in a small stream into the native slave's willing, open grave that his soul was destined to become. Straight Bear hungrily accepted the devil's blood offering, weakly at first and then with great vigor. Nvda Ama pulled his arm away from Straight Bear's lips before he collapsed to the rich dark soil, snarling and clawing. Straight Bear seemed to quit breathing, becoming rigid and still.

Then a remarkable thing happened as the three lone frightened survivors looked on. Straight Bear suddenly stood erect, breathing once again with his glazed eyes sparkled with a golden light. They had heard an eerie, crackling sound come from his bones as he stood erect. He smiled in a most devious manner. The three lone survivors discovered, to their horror, that he was slightly levitating off the ground. What was once Straight Bear now seemed to be straight from hell.

Nvda Ama looked at him with that strange golden glow in his eyes. "Welcome, my brother Straight Bear!"

Straight Bear seemed to smile even wider, if that was possible "Yes, we are surely now brothers of the same clan!" They turned at the same time toward the remaining three survivors, still smiling.

One of the survivors had a mental collapse and started mumbling nonsense. "Momma? Where are you, Momma?"

Straight Bear shushed him with a whisper and a single raised finger to his lips. "Hush, child. Your mother stands here before you." Then Straight Bear was on him with lightning speed, sinking his new long, sharp teeth into the weak mortal flesh. It tasted like paradise. The blood was likened to the sweet taste of wild honey, only more life-sustaining and satisfying. He emptied him completely and tossed him aside like a used, empty rag doll. He turned smiling to his mentor, blood still fresh upon his lips.

Nvda Ama had finished off one of the others, leaving only one left, who had scampered like a scared dog underneath one of the wagons. He was crying, begging, and praying all at once.

Straight Bear's eyes returned to normal as he looked at Nvda Ama, whose eyes had returned to normal as well. Straight Bear motioned to the soldier underneath the wagon. "And what about him?"

"Let him stay. It is time for you and I to walk a new path inside of the darkness that lives inside this world."

"I like that. Shall we?"

They turned in unison and started walking east.

The lone survivor stammered and stuttered. "Wha ... wha ... What about me?"

They stopped and turned toward him in unison, raising their right palms at him. The whole scene burst into flames like some fiery inferno from hell. The last soldier's screams grew in intensity for about ten seconds, and then all was quiet except the roaring of a fire so hot and hungry that it made the earth tremble and crack open. The smell of sulfur and brimstone poured from the earth's open wound. Even the metal parts of the wagons and horse bridles melted into a porous state and seeped into the crack in the earth, until nothing remained except the raw, scorched earth.

They both smiled at one another and dropped their palms in unison. Their eyes turned golden once again as they turned around and faded into the darkness.

A flash flood erupted from the heavens, pouring down upon the scorched earth. It extinguished the fire and filled the crack in the earth with mud until all that remained was uncharred, virgin soil. The rain ceased as the first rays of dawn showed from the east. By the time the sun had fully risen, new tiny blades of grass were already sprouting upon that virgin soil.

Epilogue

Lieutenant Dan Sanders and his twelve-member search party arrived approximately one month later, in the late afternoon. They unknowingly set up camp at that same tragic site on the east side of the Mississippi River. "Let's get ready, and set up the tents!" the lieutenant ordered the soldiers. They had been sent on a mission to investigate the mysterious disappearance of Lieutenant Carl Andrews and his small regiment.

Lieutenant Sanders silently contemplated their fate as his eyes caught a glimpse of a shiny silver object in the grass. He bent over and picked it up. It was a silver lieutenant's bar that appeared to be partially melted. "What the hell?" he said aloud, puzzled. He looked up at the evening sky. "Hurry up, men. I smell a storm upon the horizon!" And as if right on cue, small dark clouds in the east amassed. "Hurry, men! The darkness will be here soon!"

And indeed it was.

Waiting for You

I say a prayer for you, under my breath.
You are all that I have now; there is nothing left.
I feel suddenly so much older now as winter calls.
A tear stain upon your pillow as the darkness falls.
I hope life's path you chose, it treats you well
As time just drifts away into some tragic tale.
I tried to let you go; it's so damn hard.
I finally had to turn away, so bright was your star.
Where did you run away into the whispers of life's end?
I look up into the heavens and start to wonder.
I traveled between this world and another,
Reached out to touch you from my secret place.
The memory of your love never, ever fades away.
Did you feel my ghost as it caressed your soul?
I will warm your heart as this life grows cold.
Don't you cry for me—it's far too late;
I have drifted away from my earthly estate.
And I still love you forevermore.
I am waiting for you behinds death's door.

Printed in the United States
By Bookmasters

Printed in the United States
By Bookmasters